Embracing the Feminine Nature of the Divine

Integrative Spirituality Heralds the Next Phase of Conscious Evolution

by Toni G. Boehm, Ph.D.

Introduction by Andrew Harvey

Peace
Toni Boehm

First Edition 2001

Embracing the Feminine Nature of the Divine:
Integrative Spirituality Heralds
the Next Phase of Conscious Evolution

Inner Visioning Press
430 Winnebago Dr.
Greenwood, MO. 64034
816-537-5254 (F)

Published by **Inner Visioning Press**
Printed in the United States of America

The publisher wishes to gratefully acknowledge the cover design and graphic work of Gail Ishmael and the original artwork of Rev. Leslie Bradshaw. Cover art adapted from a work by Cornelius Monsma

Library of Congress Card Number: 00-191110
Embracing the Feminine Nature of the Divine / Toni G. Boehm Ph. D.
ISBN 0-9701537-1-6

1. Spirituality   2. Women's Issues   3. Body, Mind & Spirit
4. Self-Help   I. Title: Embracing the Feminine Nature of the Divine:
Integrative Spirituality Heralds the Next Phase of Conscious Evolution

⤳ Table of Contents ⤴

↜ Dedication ↝

I dedicate this book to all the women in my life, "who taught me what to do, and what not to do," I honor each of you.

To my grandmother, Annie Laurie: my mother, Eula Gene: my sisters, Rosalie and Sonny: my daughter, Michelle: my grand-daughter, Courtlyn: my special cousin, Pam: and all my other female cousins. The feminine legacy lives on WOW, isn't that a grand and scary thought! Let's each do our part to affirm the grand and transform the scary. I love you.

To Jay, who tells me daily what a wonderful person I am, by his words and actions. I am blessed by your presence in my life.

To Priscilla Richards, her love of the mystery of the Divine Feminine aided this work more than words can share.

To Rosemary Ellen Guiley, a friend and a support in the evolution of my writing skills.

To Dorothy Pierson, a grande dame, who knows who she is and what she wants. What a gift she has been in life.

To Raymond Teague, for his belief in this project and for all of the editorial wisdom he shared with me. Kudo's to Micheal Maday, also.

To Gail Ishmael, without her graphic skills this book would only be a dream.

To Eva Darbyshire, at 101 she is an example of growing older gracefully.

To Andrew Harvey, my teacher, friend, mentor and "spiritual nanny." You made a difference in my life.

To "my other" daughters, Kimberly, Allison, Amanda and Rosalyn, I am grateful for your presence in my life (and all the grandchildren you have shared with us).

✌ Foreword ↷

by

Andrew Harvey

I asked a dear friend why he worshiped the Divine Mother. The look on his face told me that he had never conceived of not worshiping her. He then took his finger and stabbed it into my shoulder, saying with a flurry of passion: "No Mother, no bone! No Mother, no bone!" His words moved me, and I understood that if there were no Mother, no motherhood of God, then there would be no creation. There would be no fish in the sea, no flowers – nothing, nowhere – for She is God in matter.

Why is it important that we, humankind, reclaim the Divine Motherhood of God? Because, without the knowledge of Divine Masculine and Feminine, without both the Mother and Father aspect of God, the human race will die out. We are disconnected, and it is only the radiance of the Mother that will heal us. She brings us the sacred connection of Oneness. We must experience Her connection as a living experience and act out of that experience.

The Mother knows unity and respects all life. We must begin to invoke Her. Different traditions know this, and it is a necessity for our species. The Divine Mother is love in action, passionate love that will not rest as long anyone goes to bed hungry or lives with the threat and fear of prejudice.

The universe is the constant, self-transforming mutual expression of the Father-Mother within the One. The universe is wet with the eternal juices of the One. The One, the Father-Mother, is the Cosmic Marriage enacted at every level.

Yet how can there be a sacred marriage when the bride is hidden – kept out of sight, hidden in the cellar of our psyche? Our work is to go into the unconscious realm of mind and learn how to heal Her. She must be brought forth to be united with the Divine Masculine.

We are ready for a revolution of the sweetest, happiest kind – one of laughter, love, and healing. I beg you to give the Divine Feminine Her due, that She might go forward in healing. Toni Boehm shared with me the following excerpt from an article printed in Unity Magazine in 1936. It was written by Charles Fillmore, cofounder of the Unity movement and Unity School of Christianity. Fillmore, perhaps one of the greatest spiritual geniuses of last two hundred years, proves to me the depth of his being with this writing.

Toni G. Boehm

In the article Mr. Fillmore reveals how the Christ force is utterly bound up with the Sacred Feminine in a very primordial way: He knew through his spiritual genius that at the core of true unity is the balance of the Divine Masculine and Divine Feminine. He came to know that without the restoration of the Sacred Feminine in all of its glory, in all of its intuition and in all of its understanding, there simply could not be Unity.

"The conception and birth of Jesus, as recorded by Luke, conceals and to the spiritually wise, reveals a soul principle that will save man from death. That Principle, represented by Mary [Jesus' mother] is Love. Up to the time of Jesus the feminine principle of the soul, love never had a chance to express itself because of the arrogant dominance of the intellect.

"Jesus would have utterly failed in the resurrection of His body after the Crucifixion, if He had not developed the restorative power of Divine love. So no man can hope to escape death until he frees the imprisoned love of his soul."

This is an amazing statement – that there is a principle that will save man from death. That principle represented by Mary is Love. In those words of Fillmore you have the beginnings, a radiant beginning of a complete theology of the Sacred Marriage – a way to open up to all the great mystical traditions about the Feminine to help you and I birth the true Christ, who is as much the son of the Mother as He is the son of Father.

My beloved friends if there is anything I could say that would be helpful, it would be this: Please see what is now at stake in the history of the planet and do everything in your power to honor, to acknowledge, to celebrate, and to be transformed by the Motherhood of God – so that the authentic and all – transforming power of the sacred marriage can at last, at long last can be expressed in you and through you.

You are the one that is open-minded enough and open-hearted enough to take this great adventure. And if you do not, you will be depriving the Christ consciousness [the Universal Presence, the balanced energy of a Mother-Father God] of one of its most potentially extraordinary vehicles. But to do so, I believe you have to do the following things:

1. I beg you to learn more about the great feminine mystics, the great mystics of the feminine in all traditions and the extraordinary work of the modern feminine mystics who are bringing in a glorious vision of the Divine Mother at this moment. And I beg you to make it a crucial priority in your life.

2. I beg you to have the courage to look without illusion at all the patri-archal ways of being, acting, teaching, structuring authority that surround you and allow them gratefully and joyfully to be transformed by the wisdom of the Mother. Invoke Her let Her heal and bring forth new structures and new forms.

3. I beg you all really to honor and celebrate women. Everywhere I go I meet quite extraordinary, passionate, radical, fiery, delicious, juicy women doing wonderful work. I don't know how many of you are aware as I am aware, that some of the most cutting edge and brilliant work on the Sacred Feminine being done now – including some of the most amazing new ritu-als for and some of the deepest theological, spiritual, and mystical explo-ration of the Sacred Feminine is being done by women they are extraordinary pioneers, and they are quite extraordinarily graceful in their acceptance of being almost silenced. And that is a sign of the depths of their spiritual maturity.

4. I am begging you to do two things for these women: acknowledge them as your true soldiers of peace and (this is directed to the men) start going to these wise women to be taught by them humbly about the Sacred Feminine.

They have tremendous wisdom for you and they can help you make the changes from the past with tremendous joy, tremendous charity, with an absence of recrimination and resentment – because in their hearts I have discovered no resentment and no recrimination. Go to them, because they contain the secret of the transformation and they can help you make it – radiantly and beautifully. Celebrate the women, in your midst, who are extraordinary repositories of the wisdom of the Mother and who are doing extraordinary work on the Sacred Feminine.

Let us look at something that is at the core of why the Feminine has been so despised. The Feminine is despised fundamentally because it cuts shorts and balances our fantasies of transcendence by presenting to us the facts of the body, death, and the shadow – because in the Feminine aspect of the Godhead, darkness is as holy as light, suffering is as essential as joy, and everything that we describe as profane is in fact lit up with electric, mystical meaning.

So, my friends, the light and the dark must make love within you, joy and suffering must make love within you, and all aspects of all the opposites must be acknowledged. This is at present damped by an overemphasis on

Toni G. Boehm

the light, which is in fact in its most secret part motivated by fear – the fear of dying, the fear of the body, the fear of pain, the fear of actually taking on the responsibility of being the living Christ in this world. And for this fear the most powerful heroine is an addiction to the light yourself. At the core of us is a tremendous fear of the Divine Feminine. Address the fear. Open yourself to the Divine Feminine and let Her heal you.

Say yes to darkness, yes to light, yes to suffering, yes to joy, yes to immanence, yes to transcendence, yes to life, yes to death, yes to breaking down the walls of death.

Who is a person in the service of the Christ, the balanced energy of the Mother-Father God?

1. He or she is a cradle of welcome, a place where beings of all kinds – whether black or white or yellow or gay or straight – can feel the mercy and the forgiveness of God.

2. He or she is a crucible of Divine Love and who is willing to share that Love with the world through service.

3. He or she is serving the Christ consciousness as an enormous, highly polished, and brilliantly transparent lens through which the light of Divine Justice, straight from the heart of the Father-Mother, can be focused on the real agony, the real struggle, of the real world to free the whole human race from oppression.

In the Mother's Love,
Andrew Harvey

ꙮ Introduction: Thoughts to Ponder ꙮ

"At the very dawn of religion,
God was a woman. Do you remember?"
—Merlin Stone *When God Was a Woman*

The first time I read these words about a feminine nature of the Divine, something on a cellular level resonated to their sound as I spoke them aloud. An energy vibrated throughout my being. From asking this question, other questions surfaced, and they would not leave me alone. From a place deep within me, I wanted to understand. What happened to Her? What was Her story? If there is a movement going on around the return of the Divine Mother, when did it begin? What does the archetypal energy of the feminine face of God have to offer me, personally and to humankind in total? Each question birthed another question and they became the crux of my inquiry and the foundation of my quest.

If one looks closely, at the journey of the **feminine nature of the Divine** (This **feminine nature** has also been known by such names as the Divine Mother, the Divine Feminine, Goddess, Mother Earth, Gaia, Divine Ancestress, and so on. **The Divine** is also called the One, Source, Universal Energy, Spirit, Higher Power, Cosmic Energy, and so forth.) what they will discover is that "She" has been for the past several millennia, sent into exile and held captive in the deep recesses of the subconscious mind. However, by all appearances, this feminine nature of the Divine now seems to be making Her way out of the dark caverns of the subconscious mind, into the light of conscious awareness.

It could be said that there has been an underground movement which has been swelling, rising and gaining conscious momentum. This movement appears to be directed toward the reclaiming and restoring the feminine nature of the Divine to the right and perfect place in the consciousness of humankind. As we entered the new millennium, this movement began to take on the stirrings of an even stronger and more powerful force.

However, the long term result of this banishment from conscious awareness is that the archetypal energy of the feminine nature of the Divine has become a part of the "shadow" of the collective consciousness of humankind. For by dividing God Energy into two separate halves and in essence ordering, through religious ideology, the upholding of one half to

Toni G. Boehm

the exclusion of the other, what this has done to the psyche of humankind is to condemn human beings to a state of feeling incomplete and not whole. Worse yet, they do not understand why they feel this way and without conscious awareness, the unconscious content of the subconscious mind is forced to play itself out by way of compulsive acts performed by the adverse aspect of the ego. This acting out is also known as "shadow" behavior.

Personally and collectively, the shadow is the emotional residue of our past experiences that have been repressed or hidden under a "veneer of social decorum" – the layer of beliefs that we hold that have been defined according to the conditioning we received from our family, teachers, preachers, priests, culture, society, and social mores, values and customs.

Not only did we and do we hide our emotional residue, but in order to protect ourselves from the information that it holds, we take our residue and we project it onto others as if they were in reality theirs, when in fact it is ours.

For example, a person has a history of being abandoned and has never faced the depth of the pain he or she carries with regard to this issue. What tends to happen over time is that all the unresolved emotional residue around the abandonment issue, the memories, thoughts, and feelings, gets denied. In other words, the abandonment issue is not dealt with consciously because it is too painful. So, the easiest thing to do is to hide the issue. Thus, through the action of denial, this emotional residue gets repressed into the subconscious mind. Therefore, rather than facing the issue and embracing it consciously, in the "light of day," it is denied and repressed, and banished deeper into the subconscious mind.

Repressed emotional energy – and thoughts are energy – doesn't go anywhere. Instead the repressed energy takes on a new form. It begins to reveal itself in another way, which is usually acted out unconsciously through our behaviors and/or projected onto others (this repressed energy can reveal itself in a myriad of reactions or dysfunctional behaviors in us, such as – jealousy, anger, greed, lying, anxiety disorders, addictions, etc.).

Consciously, we do not "own" that we have an issue or problem and the tendency is to project the repressed energy that we carry around our issues onto someone else. When we engage in projection, we believe the real problem is with the other person, instead of our self.

We usually tend to see the other persons foibles or "misgivings" so clearly. We say that that person is so <u>fill-in the blank</u>, (fearful, jealous, afraid, anxious, obnoxious, angry, untrust-worthy, etc.) Projection is "an involuntary transfer of our own unconscious behaviors onto others, so that it appears to us that these qualities actually exist in the other people." Thus we can see clearly when other people act in a jealous manner, yet we rationalize that our jealous behavior is not jealousy at all, but a justified act of "protecting" our territory from others who are out to get what is ours or to do harm to us. (This is a very simplistic overview.)

This same type of scenario has been happening in the consciousness of humankind for the past several millennia. The repression of the feminine nature of the Divine by humankind has created over time a "hole of denial" in the fabric of human consciousness. This hole of denial has revealed itself in behaviors and ideology such as; the inabilities to treat women — and others perceived as less-than's — as equals; a disregard for equality in human life; ideas that condone sexual supremacy for the male species; the need to own and possess other people; hierarchal way's of doing life and business; the need to control another's life which is played out through acts of sexual mutilation; a need to change other peoples views, culture and mores in order that they become aligned with the "right way"; a refusal to allow women to hold positions of high authority within religious establishments; and so on. If left unrepaired this hole of denial will ultimately create a rent in the fabric of humankind's consciousness that may not be repairable.

We can no longer, as individuals and as a society, patch this hole with platitudes or overtures of goodwill. Consciousness must be rewoven at its deepest levels using the threads of the attributes of the Divine Mother aspect of Cosmic Energy. For Hers are the threads which hold a binding quality and which are able to connect us consciously, heart to heart. Using Her threads of love, unity, faith, interconnectedness, equality, balance, respect, authority, fearlessness, comfort with the unknown, the mystery in life, and so forth, humankind can reweave the fabric of consciousness to its original state of spiritual wholeness. And that is what the spiritual journey is all about – returning us to our original state of oneness in the One.

Using the analogy of reweaving, three major threads of thought came forth to unfold Her story in book form. The first thread begins at the dawn of religion, when the feminine face of God reigned. It continues to unravel until we come to the appearance of Her ultimate demise through forced repression. With the second thread, we see how the hole of denial punctured the fabric of human consciousness, as we review the ensuing problems that have arisen in the psyche of humankind. The third thread is a thread of

Toni G. Boehm

hope, for it contains the essence of Her message as to how humankind can begin the healing and transformation of consciousness, personally and collectively.

I believe that the time of conscious repression of the feminine nature of the Divine is over and that the feminine aspect is now coming forth out of the hidden recesses of the collective unconscious of humankind, as a shining example of the Motherhood of God. Although Her movement from the hidden to the "known" is slow and laborious, those who are aware of Her true splendor and majesty are reveling in each millimeter of awareness that is coming forth.

My deepest desire for you is that you may awaken to the glory of the feminine nature of the Divine in you and to all the gifts that it has to offer. For when the Feminine energy in you, begins to work in tandem with the Masculine energy, you will have the "spiritual keys" to unlock the energetic potential that leads to the full regeneration of your mind and body.

In our Divinity we are androgynous beings, both masculine and feminine in nature. This is what the man known as, Jesus Christ, came to teach humankind. For it is said that he came not to abolish the law (the masculine nature) but to fulfill it (make it whole) through Love and Grace (the feminine nature).

As you begin to stroll through the pages of this book, reading the words that the Divine Mother has placed upon my heart, I invite you to search your heart to see if you hold any preconceived judgments about the feminine nature of the Divine. If you find that you do, I ask you to surrender them for just a few moments.

Many of the quotes that you will find throughout this book come from the leaders of the New Thought movement. One of the founders of this movement, was the twentieth-century mystic Charles Fillmore, cofounder of Unity School of Christianity. Fillmore was well aware of the feminine nature of the Divine and of the importance of these qualities in the regeneration process. His writings are full of thoughts about "Her" work that are as fresh, original, and contemporary as they would be if they were being written today. For example:

UNITY'S STATEMENT OF FAITH
February 12, 1921 – Weekly Unity
Statement #16

*"I believe that the Holy Mother, the Divine Feminine,
is now being restored to her righteousness in the world
and that she will reign equal with
Jehovah [the Divine Masculine]
in the heavens and the earth."*

— Charles and Myrtle Fillmore

Toni G. Boehm

↜ Reweaving the Fabric of Human Consciousness ↝
Thread I:

The Historical Perspective of the Initial Rise and Ultimate Repression of the Feminine nature of the Divine

Thread I (which includes Chapters 1 through 3) is woven with historical strands taken from as long ago as 50,000 B. C. E. and continuing through the New Thought movement and up to the modern era. These chapters traverse the historical path of the rise and ultimate repression of the Feminine face of God.

Archeological evidence has been found of a time when God was thought to be a woman, and it is believed that the people of these ancient times stood in awe of the creative powers a woman held. Although this idea of a God with a Feminine face, reigned for tens of thousands of years, somehow this aspect of our spiritual, physiological, social, and psychological history has been repressed or forgotten.

Reflecting upon these thoughts, the questions that arise include these: How or why did we, a collective society, forget this aspect of God? What was the causative factor that led to the repression of this ancient memory? The next important question is, how do we, as a collective whole, begin to remember?

"Wholeness ... is not achieved
by cutting off a portion of one's being,
but by an integration of the contraries."
– Carl Jung

✦ Chapter One ✦

Where Has "She" Gone?

"Why is it important that we, humankind,
reclaim the Divine Motherhood of God?
Because, without the knowledge of Divine Masculine and Feminine,
without both the Mother and Father aspect of God, the
human race will die out.
We are disconnected and it is only the radiance of the
Mother that will heal us.
She brings us the sacred connection of Oneness.
We must experience Her connection
as a living experience and act out of that experience."
–Andrew Harvey, *Mary's Vineyard*

Once upon a time – long, long ago – the feminine nature of the divine lived and took form in the body and shape of a woman. People held this thought because they stood in awe of the creative powers that a woman held because she was able to use a mysterious power within her body to create new life. Although this idea of a feminine nature of the divine existed for tens of thousands of years, somehow this part of our spiritual history has been forgotten. How or why did we forget? And more importantly how do we begin to remember?

Interestingly enough, the twentieth-century began the journey to remembering, for during this time a potential societal, religious, and life-changing phenomenon occurred. That phenomenon was the discovery of ancient images depicting God in a Feminine form. These ancient images, coming from a variety of cultures provided us with tangible, visual reflections of an early religion or spirituality in which the source of life was provided by and through a Mother-God figure, the Divine Feminine.

It seems that these images may have the possibility of redefining the face of religion as we have known it for the past four thousand years or more, for they are recalling a remembrance that lives deep in our cellular memories. And with each layer of memory that is uncovered, we are taken more fully into the awareness of who we are as spiritual beings. Remembering that we are made in the image and likeness of God. *"Let us make humankind in our image, according to our likeness; .... So ... male and female he created them. "* [Gen. 1:26-27, NRSV]

Toni G. Boehm

These visual images, the oldest of which dates back to 35,000 B.C.E., have been found in France, Malta, Siberia, Mexico, and many other parts of the world. Whether hidden in caves, drawn on walls, cut into mountains, or made into pottery figurines and whether carved on bone, stone, and ivory, these likenesses of the face of a Feminine Deity provide us with an astonishing new description of God. Most of us have been raised with a male-only face of God, and the unveiling of these discoveries makes us stop, take a breath, and ask: "Could it be that the story of the beginning of humankind and its religious roots did not evolve as we have been led to believe? Could there be another story?"

Please note: Throughout this book, within quotes the words contained within the brackets [ ] and <u>not</u> in *italics* are my personal clarifications.

One of the first writers of the last century on the Divine Feminine and the Motherhood of God, Mary Esther Harding, says in her book *Women's Mysteries* that *"**She was known under different names in different countries and in different ages, but her life story, her attributes and characteristics, did not vary very greatly even though the name of the religion changed from place to place.**"*

Testimonies from ancient cultures are now revealing to us that this is the truth. These validations from the far past show us that a multifaceted, powerful Feminine-based spirituality existed within these cultures. This Feminine-based spirituality spanned the time from approximately 35,000 to 1000 B.C.E., albeit after 4,000 B.C.E. Feminine-based spirituality was in decline.

This Divine Feminine face took the shape of images such as Ishtar, the Great Mother goddess of Mesopotamia and Babylonia; Isis, the goddess-queen of the Egyptian civilization; Gaia, from classical Greece; Kali, from India; Kuan Yin, from China; Chalchiuhtlicue, from Mexico; the Goddess of Willendorf, from Austria; the Goddess of Laussel, from France; Spider Woman, from North America; and Ala and Ochen, from Africa. These are just a few of the many feminine Deities that are known to have been worshiped thousands and thousands of years ago.

Then – as all things must in the cycle of birth, death, and rebirth – things began to change. Feminine-based spirituality – with its attributes of sharing, natural healing, intuition, equality, the love of nature, peace-filled living, and the honoring of all life began to be replaced with a masculine-based spirituality that honored the masculine attributes of power, (which when abused leads to a desire for power over others), intelligence, and hierarchal ways of living.

Around 4500 B.C.E. the Bronze Age was ushered in. With it came the ability to make weapons. This new technology seemed to create within the psyche of humankind a thirst for power. "Power over" everything became the conscious and unconscious cry of human consciousness. The masculine-dominated thought forms of a hierarchal type of society replaced the feminine-dominated thought forms of a more collective society.

The "patriarchal inversion" is the name that was given to this plunge into the abyss of change and destruction. Consciousness began to shift from a matri-focal society to a patri-focal one, and the expression of the Feminine face of God had no place or say within it. Susan Cahill, in her book *Wise Women*, says of this experience that *"the Mother Goddess ... was gradually replaced with a Father God who became the patriarchal God of the Israelites, the Christians, and the Muslims, the focus of male-dominant theologies."*

Sophia-Wisdom, A Hypostate of God

Cahill says: *"The feminine was not completely suppressed in [early] Judaism, however. It figures in the notion of Shekinah as the female aspect of God or the name for the manifestation of the sacred presence on earth in the cloud and fire ... the burning bush ... It appears, too in the figure of Hokhmah, the Hebrew embodiment of Wisdom – like the Greek Sophia, feminine in gender."*

In the Hebrew Testament references to this Judaic, feminine nature of the divine – Wisdom, or (as She was known in the Greek) Sophia – are found in Proverbs, Ecclesiastes, and the Song of Solomon.

Let me note that it is from the name Sophia that the word *philosophy*, the "love of Sophia," was coined. Allow me to share with you the true meaning that underlies the concept of the "love of Sophia" philosophy. *Sophia* in Greek, means "Wisdom"; *philosophy* means "the love of Wisdom."

Robert Powell, in his book *Trinosophia*, shares the story of how the coining of the word *philosophy* came about. In approximately 600 B.C.E., there lived a Greek philosopher named Pythagorus; he is considered to be the father of mathematics and was also recognized as a profound religious teacher.

Pythagorus taught that Sophia-Wisdom, or philosophy, was a way of learning which comes from going within and tapping the source of the divine Mother who resides within one's heart. However, over the centuries, Pythagorus' deeper meaning of the word *philosophy* was lost and it became replaced with or understood as an abstract way of gleaning knowledge from outer sources. Now, back to Sophia-Wisdom in the Judaic culture.

Sophia was considered a hypostate of God, a personified attribute of God. Sophia grew in religious and societal stature and importance from the 4th to the 1st century (B.C.E. refers to the time before the birth of Jesus Christ.) Joan Chamberlain Engelsman, in *The Feminine Demension of the Divine*, says she believes that Sophia had become such an influential figure that her power rivaled any Hellenistic Goddess but Sophia expressed God in a different way from that of the Goddesses of Hellenistic Greece and Egypt, for She had no separate cult or independent status. She was an attribute of God. Although much was written about the feminine nature of the divine in the Hebrew Testament, very little is ever taught about it. What do you remember being taught about the Feminine face of God, Wisdom, or Sophia as a child?

Wisdom-Sophia in Judaism is found in the Wisdom Literature; the Canons, the Apocrypha, and the Psuedepigrapha. You can find references to Wisdom in the books of Proverbs (see Chapters 1-9, circa 3rd and 4th century B.C.E.), in Ben Sirach or Ecclesiastics (circa 2nd century B.C.E.), and in the Wisdom of Solomon (circa 1st century B.C.E.). (These are approximate dates of the writing of these texts.)

Here are a few references that show Her glory and honor:

"Furthermore, being One, She can do all things and remaining in Herself, She renews all things." – *Wisdom Literature 7:27*

"I am wisdom, my neighbor is intelligence, I am found in (company with) knowledge and thought." – *Proverbs 8:22* and *8:12-33*

"Wisdom praises herself, and is honored among her people." – *Ben Sirach 24:1-31*

King Solomon speaks of her with admiration;

"For there is in Her a spirit quick of understanding, holy, alone in kind." – *Wisdom of Solomon 7:22 - 8:1*

In the book *Wisdom's Feast* (written by Cole, Ronan and Taussig), the writers make the point that Sophia, as She is described in Proverbs, portrays a dual perspective. She is valiantly trying to subvert prostitution and promote family life, yet there is also an underlying theme of oppression toward women. Cole, et al, *"We must admit that the society within which Sophia emerged was patriarchal. At certain points in the Sophia texts then, Sophia is part of an interlocking system of symbols which were used to confirm women's subordinate place in society ... She served dual functions, both liberating and oppressing women in the particular social contexts of her emergence."*

Another point that is made by several writers is the idea that if you highlight all of the times a reference is made to an aspect of the Feminine face of God in the Hebrew Testament, it far exceeds the mention of Abraham, Isaac, Jacob, Moses, and Isaiah; yet this Feminine face of God is rarely spoken of or referred to.

These feminine references include the following:

a. *El Shaddai* – El Shaddai is mentioned approximately forty-eight times throughout the Hebrew Testament and in Hebrew, El Shaddai, has a very feminine connotation, for *Shad* means "breast" and *ai* is a word ending that refers to the feminine.

Charles Fillmore shared many thoughts about the feminine nature of the divine in a 1930s series of articles that he combined and entitled, *"The Hidden Man of the Bible."* Many of the 19 articles comprising this series, were used by Fillmore in Sunday lessons and published as *Unity Magazine* articles. The first sharing used here was entitled, *"The Cooperation of the Christ and the Holy Spirit,"* it was published in 1939. The second piece was called, *"The Hidden Man of the Bible: Almighty God."*

In *" ... Christ and the Holy Spirit,"* Fillmore shares his thoughts about the meaning of *El Shaddai*. Fillmore says: *"Although there are many splendid feminine characters in the Bible they are so submerged by the quantity of the masculine that their creative importance is seldom mentioned. Even where the feminine companion of Jehovah, El-Shaddai, is mentioned her identity is covered up by a totally inaccurate translation, 'Almighty.' Scofield, an accepted authority in Hebrew literature says that wherever in the Bible the word Almighty occurs it should read, 'El-Shaddai,' which means 'the breasted one,' or wife; that is, the divine feminine ... Christianity has been personalized and masculinized to death... Woman is failing to measure up to her Divine type because of the picture of her physical origin which is being carried in the race consciousness."*

In the *" ... Almighty God"* piece Fillmore shares: *"It was on every account to be regretted that "Shaddai' was translated 'Almighty.' ... The etymological signification of Almighty God, (El Shaddai) is both interesting and touching. God (El) signifies the Strong One. The qualifying noun Shaddai [means] the breast, invariably used in Scripture for a woman's breast. Shaddai therefore means primarily 'the breasts.'* [This would mean that *El Shaddai* could be interpreted as the *Strong One with Breasts*, which is exactly the image the Paleolithic and Neo-lithic people carried of *The Great Mother, The Divine Ancestress.*]

"In the seventeenth chapter of Genesis is the first appearance of El Shaddai where, as God almighty She announces to Abram that She will make him the Father of a multitude of nations, also because of the fecundity which She gave him he would no longer be called Abram but Abraham ... Abraham's wife Sarai was ninety years of age but El Shaddai, the Divine Mother, promised that she should bring forth a son"

b. The word **Yahweh** also has a very feminine association. Here Yahweh is used in a manner that suggests that God has a maternal or womb-like quality. *"You forgot the God who gave you birth"* (Deut. 32:18 RSV).

c. In the Hebrew Testament, the word for Spirit or Holy Spirit – Rhuah or Ruah – is mentioned almost four hundred times. Its meaning is said to suggest *"the life of God or essence through which the Divine acts."* It was this essence of God that eventually became known as Wisdom and is also referred to in the Kabbalah by the feminine name **Hokhmah**.

For me the questions become: If there are all these references to a Feminine Face of God in the Bible, then how did "She" get lost? What happened to Her? Where did we lose Her?

The Role of Philo, the Philosopher

Similar references to the reason behind the demise of Sophia are set forth by authors: Joan Engelsman, in *The Feminine Dimension of the Divine;* Catlin Matthews, in *Sophia, Goddess of Wisdom;* and Robert Powell, in his tapes *Sophia's Teachings.* It is thought that a major player in the eclipse of the feminine nature of the divine was Philo, the philosopher. Philo was born several years prior to Christ and died in 60 A.D. Philo was a teacher, philosopher, and writer and he was very well respected for his philosophical views, yet his disdain for anything feminine was very evident in his writings. Engelsman shares the following words from Philo regarding Wisdom-Sophia, women in general, and ultimately the Feminine Face of God:

"While Wisdom's name is feminine, her nature is manly. For that which comes after God occupies a second place and therefore was termed feminine to express contrast with the maker who is masculine. For preeminence always pertains to the masculine and the feminine always comes short of and is lesser than it." (Philo – Fuga, 50-52)

"For progress is indeed nothing else than giving up of the female gender by changing [her] into the male. The Female is material, passive, corporeal, and sense perception, while the Male is active, rational, incorporeal and more akin to mind and thought." (Philo – QEI, 8)

The Divine Feminine threatened Philo, He treated Her as though She were an opponent to be conquered. His range of influence was so considerable that his writings affected the creation and shape of newly forming tenets and dogma of Christianity.

These next points are a summary of Engelsman's thoughts regarding the impact that Philo's writings had on engendering an anti-feminine train of thought into the newly developing Christian theology:

1. Philo sowed the seeds for the overt repression of all things regarded as feminine, "either philosophically or physically." This repression of the feminine laid the foundation for the thought form that eventually became Christian theology, with the masculine aspect of God being the common reference.

2. Philo took the significant feminine attributes of Wisdom-Sophia and gave them a masculine bent. By shifting them into a masculine context, Philo succeeded in setting the stage for the Wisdom's attributes to be transferred to the masculine figure of the Logos – Jesus Christ.

An example of a change that appears to be a direct effect of Philo's influence can be found in the Gospel of John. It is the shift from Sophiology to Christology. But before we go there, let us travel back in time for a moment to a song of exaltation and praise (an aretalogy) that was written in the second century B.C.E. This aretalogy is entitled *"The Cyme"*:

"I am Isis, mistress of the land. I am eldest daughter ... I am wife ... I am she that riseth ... I divided earth and heaven ... I am Queen of rivers ... I am war ... I am the rays in the sun ... With me everything is reasonable (possible?) ... I set free those in bonds ... I am Lord."

Do these "I am" statements sound familiar? Not only were they used to describe Sophia in the Hebrew Testament, they were used in Egypt to describe Isis. Both were feminine-type deities reigning during the same time period. However, the writer of John takes these words and transfers the powers and attributes of the feminine deity to the masculine Logos and then identifies Christ as the incarnate Logos. Thus Christ becomes the Word made flesh, the I Am, Wisdom.

For example, Wisdom 7:26, 29: *"She is an effulgence from everlasting light"* In John 8:12: *"I am the light of the world."*

Other images that were used in pre-Christian times to describe Wisdom-Sophia but got transferred to the Christ include living water, bread, true vine, and good shepherd. Engelsman also shares that the caring, nurturing aspect of the feminine dimension of Jesus is expressed in many stories in John but they only appear in this Gospel.

For example, His countenance of respect, sensitivity, and compassion toward women is very evident in this Gospel. At Cana, He moves from being a little irritated at his mother to being open and receptive toward her council, when she tells Him that He "can" turn the water into wine. His protective side comes forth with Mary Magdalene at the anointing, when Judas is chastising her for wasting precious ointment. Again, with Mary Magdalene, He shows His gentle side with her at the tomb – when He lovingly says her name. Immediately she recognizes Him through the sound of His voice. The fact that Mary Magdalene (a woman) is the first person He chooses to reveal Himself to in His risen body shows deep respect for her and for women. Then there is the Samaritan woman: He confides in her that He is the Christ, the Messiah – when He had as yet told no one else.

Paul – in 1 Corinthians 2:6-8; 1:24, 30; and in other scriptures – uses Wisdom-Sophia language to speak about Jesus. Terms and concepts that came from the ancient Wisdom Schools are now used to supplant Wisdom-Sophia's authority and give it to Jesus.

The leaders of the newly forming Christianity took Philo's words and created a dogma that left the feminine nature of the divine out. But why did they do this? Was there a hidden reason behind this decision? There is much speculation regarding this question; however, it is conjectured that it was influenced by the "Gnostic controversy." Developing Christianity had two or more veins of thought vying for the right to be the foundational premise of this newly forming religion. One prominent one was the Gnostic vein of thought, and another was one I will call the Orthodox view.

Gnosticism proclaimed Jesus as Wisdom-Sophia, as carrier of the feminine nature of the divine. They also believed it was the inner knowledge, or Gnosis [meaning hidden wisdom which the feminine represents], that Jesus tapped into which saved humanity, and not the act of the crucifixion. This view had as its underpinning the idea that not only Jesus could do this, but that all of humankind could – and without the help of an intercessory. This is a very important religious concept, or tenet, when the competition is setting up a religion based on the intercession of the souls of the common people by the religious leaders. Gnosticism also allowed for and had a very strong female presence within the ranks of their leadership.

Validation of the strong Gnostic and feminine presence in early Christianity has been discovered in a collection of writings found in 1945 in a cave in Nag Hammadi, Egypt. Known as the Nag Hammadi Library or Gnostic Gospels, these particular texts are thought to have been circulated around 150 C.E.

These Gnostic writings present God in a context of "both/and," both as a Mother and a Father God. In the Gospel of Thomas, Jesus Christ speaks of *"My Mother, the Spirit."* It is proclaimed in various logions (scriptures) from the Nag Hammadi Library that Mary Magdalene was a disciple of this Gnostic tradition. However, none of these Gnostic Gospels were accepted into the Canonical Gospels, or the Orthodox version of the Bible.

The other major vein of thought was held by a more traditional or orthodox group (undoubtedly influenced by Philo's writings and later by others such as Augustine, Tertullian, and Constantine). This other group set forth the premise that Jesus was our Savior and that He died and suffered for our sins – sins for which we could repent, but only with the aid of an assigned agent of the church. This set up a hierarchal type of system within religion.

The "big break" for the more orthodox strain of Christianity came when the emperor Constantine converted to its beliefs in 312 C.E. Constantine's conversion is said to have occurred through the influence of his mother Helena, who had already converted to the Christian teachings. (Isn't it interesting that it was a feminine influence – Helena – that led the way for the spread of Christianity worldwide?) Once converted, Constantine, being one who liked a hierarchal system, leaned in the direction of the more orthodox strain of Christian teachings.

The religious leaders of the newly forming Christianity – in order to get

Constantine's blessing, monetary support, and influence, which would help carry Christianity across the world – chose to veer far away from any type of reference to a feminine nature of the divine and more toward the orthodox, hierarchal positioning. They did not in any way want to appear as if they were siding with the Gnostic view of spirituality. This was the "final nail in Her coffin." The Christological debates in the third and fourth centuries ended with Jesus assuming the position of the Son of God, and any reference to the feminine nature of the divine, Sophia-Wisdom , or Gnostic-type influence was discarded.

"The Feminine Holocaust"

Yet even after the Christian religion was well rooted and established, the religious establishment was still quite afraid of women and of the Feminine-based spirituality concepts. Eventually their fear became so profound that the religious establishment began to call any woman who had and used the knowledge and secrets of the feminine-based spirituality, a "witch." The religious leaders said that the teachings and sacred wisdom around the use of herbs for healing, midwifery, cycles of the moon, speaking out from one's own truth about God, and so on were sacrilege and went against the church's teachings.

Because these women were perceived as such a threat, it was decided that they must be gotten rid of. "Burn her at the stake" it was said the religious leaders cried out, "for her ways are strange and could possibly hurt us. She has powerful magic which she can turn against us."

Burn her for her "strange" beliefs and wisdom? Yes! Although the numbers vary, it is thought that perhaps hundreds of thousands of women were tortured and/or burned at the stake for their beliefs in a more feminine-based spirituality. For three hundred years these atrocities went on. Midwives, herbalists, healers – women known to have sacred knowledge – were all targeted, tortured, and burned. Teacher and lecturer Jean Shinoda Bolen has labeled this time of burning a "feminine holocaust." This feminine holocaust cemented women's future in society and in religion, and this negative typecasting has lasted for centuries.

I find it very interesting that after the commencement of this feminine holocaust, the next period of human evolution was called "The Dark Ages."

꩜ Chapter Two ꩜

"Let Us Make Them in Our Image"

*"These Great Mothers whose worship
has dominated the religious thoughts of peoples
far removed from each other in time, space, and culture,
have an essential similarity which cannot but amaze us."*
—Mary Esther Harding
Women's Mysteries

Hermes Trismegistus, often called the father of alchemy, wrote the following words thousands of years ago: *"As above, so below."* This means that what is alive and happening in the realm of the heavens is reflected and replicated on the earth plane also.

In the *Hebrew Testament*, Genesis 1:26-27, a similar theme is brought to life when the Creator sets forth a decision to reflect itself into the world, saying, "Let us make them in our image ... So ... *male and female he created them."* (NRSV) In these few words the desire of the One to reflect and replicate Itself is set forth.

We find in the *Tao Te Ching*, written by Lao Tse more than five thousand years ago, another example of this desire of the One to reflect Itself. It says:

*"Before heaven and earth existed,
there was [the One] something unformed, silent, alone,
unchanging, constant and eternal;
It could be called 'the Source of the Universe'
The Nameless {Tao} is the Father of heaven and earth;
that which is named {Te} is the Mother of all things.
These two are the same; they are given different names
in order to distinguish between them.
Together they constitute the Supreme Mystery."*

And from the ancient Egyptians, this same thought is repeated:

Toni G. Boehm

"...there was a time when neither heaven nor earth existed and when nothing had being except the boundless primeval water. At length, the Spirit of the primeval water felt the desire for creative activity, and having uttered the word, the world sprang straightway into being in the form which had already been depicted in the mind of the Spirit before he spake the word which resulted in its creation."

– Sir Wallis Budge, *God's of the Egyptian's*

This creation story is repeated over and over throughout various religions: the One contains the Two, different but similar entities. Both aspects contain the essence of the One, but reflect It in different ways, qualities, and polarities. This One, reflecting Itself as the two polarities of humankind, we have come to know as the masculine and feminine natures of the divine. These two, working together, are said to comprise the "Supreme Mystery of Life" – a "Supreme Mystery" that contains within it the ability to sustain Itself and to cocreate with, in, and through Itself.

The Law of Gender

The law of gender basically states that it takes two polarities, two opposite sides of a continuum, to come together to create a third entity. It takes a mother and a father to create a child, which is the masculine and feminine coming together to birth the next generation; it takes light and dark to birth the fullness of a day; water and hydrogen to birth oxygen; red and yellow to birth orange. Waves of energy come from the creative darkness of the universe to join with the light of conscious human awareness to birth a thought, and the possibility for combination goes on and on.

But what happens when there is only one segment or aspect that is recognized and honored? I believe the answer to the question is that unbalanced energy results – mental, physical, emotional, and spiritual energy which elicits in consciousness a sense of separation within the being, rather than a sense of wholeness and balance. In this sense of separation, we wander in a wilderness of chaotic activity, desiring to know who we are and yet projecting the accomplishment of that desire onto others. Our mating call is, "Join with me and make me feel whole." Somehow we get lulled into believing that someone else or something else will help us quench the gnawing feeling which lives inside us – a feeling which wants to know completeness and balance and yet, no matter how hard we try, the "outer stuff" is never the right thing.

Fillmore shares his opinion on this idea of spiritual wholeness in an article from *Unity Magazine* in September 1935 entitled *"The Hidden Man of the Bible: "Woman"* He says: ***"Regardless of claims of infallibility for sacred writings on the part of their champions, we should remember that they were all produced by human hands and that they are all tinctured by the human minds through which they came ... The books that were left out of our Bible may be inspiring and the sincere seeker for Truth may find answers to his questions in the Apocrypha that are not in the Authorized Version ... We note particularly that the Apocryphal scriptures give prominence to the feminine side of the "hidden man," which our Authorized Bible submerges in the achievements of the masculine man.***

"Although the 1st chapter of Genesis plainly sets forth that Elohim God created man in his image and likeness – "male and female created He them" – the compilers of the great Book have virtually ignored woman as having a vital part in the divine plan. The three hundred and eighteen bishops at the council of Nice were all men and their God was a he-man. As women have demanded and gained a voice in the management of affairs of state so they will at a not far-distant future demand a new and more generous compilation of sacred writings, in which the female shall have equal place with the male. When this is accomplished, many of the fine books found in the Apocrypha will undoubtedly be incorporated into the new Bible and the "hidden feminine" be revealed.

"So we who are seeking the 'hidden man' of the Bible will never find him until we discern him to be male and female ... The masculine phase of mind has been allowed to dominate so long that it now assumes that everything must be subservient to it and that its dominion and dictation is the edict of divine law. The feminine, with its mighty heritage of love, has been mesmerized into this belief and accepts as a matter of course the rule of head over the heart. This false state of mind has thrown the whole race out of balance and severed the spiritual connecting link between man and God, which is love ... Jesus Christ was a balanced combination of wisdom and love, masculine and feminine."

Toni G. Boehm

The Feminine Nature of the Divine and Paganism

For the past several thousand years, in consciousness, a part of us, our feminine nature, has been forgotten and repressed and it has cost us dearly, as a personal and collective society and in consciousness. We have lost, set aside, and forgotten a segment of who we are as the Divine, and this loss has taken a toll on the psyche of humankind and the planet. We, humankind, are out of balance in consciousness, and it is being reflected in our lives, in our weather, in the earth's movements, and in a multitude of other ways.

How do we begin to reclaim this lost or forgotten aspect of ourselves? How do we begin to regain our balance? The answer is quite simple – by consciously choosing to bring the Feminine Face of God back into remembrance; by refusing to let the feminine nature of the divine go unnoticed and unrecognized any longer; by consciously choosing to experience what I like to call integrative spirituality — a spirituality that has successfully integrated both aspects of God into it.

In order to spark and ignite the fire of remembrance within you, there is an idea or question that I would like to present to you for your consideration:

This question is one that I often get asked during women's retreats or seminars. It is, "Why would I want to reclaim the Divine Feminine as a part of my life, when its culture, tradition, and history appear to have a pagan connotation?" I usually answer this question in the following manner: "Yes, it does appear that way, but where does the word pagan come from and what does it really mean?"

Here is a short synopsis of the history of the word *pagan*. *Pagan* means "country dwellers." Hundreds (and possibly thousands) of years ago, people were given the label "pagan" because they lived in the country and were not sophisticated. The pagans lived off the land, they knew the secrets of nature and of the earth, and they respected the earth as a feminine aspect of the divine. They knew that the earth was a part of the Great Mother.

The Mother gave of Her bounty to Her children, through the cycles of the season and through birth, life, and death – and the children understood this. She was birth and the spirit of life, She was growth and ripeness, and She was death – the end of a cycle of life. The country dwellers knew this and lived in comfort with these ideas; however, most city-dwelling people were not educated in this country lore or ways. These city folks misunderstood the country-dwelling people and their spiritual traditions. The citified considered their pagan, country-dwelling cousins' ways a bit unorthodox.

For instance, do you know how the concept of a "witch riding a broom" came about? It is said to have started like this: The country dwellers or pagans, every spring at the first full moon before the crops were planted, would take a broom to the field and sweep the land. This was done as part of a sacred ritual that honored the Great Mother and was meant to show Her that Her blessing of an abundant crop was greatly appreciated. It was believed that the sweeping would remove any negative energy or varmints and that it would help stir up the sacred energy contained within the land. This stirring up of the energy would bless the land and bring forth a bountiful crop.

Often, while doing this, the people would become so energized that they would jump on the broom and prance and dance around. To an outsider, especially a city dweller who did not understand the way of the land and of nature, this activity when seen out of context would appear to be something that was strange, weird, and possibly frightening. This ritual became misunderstood and rumors began to fly that the country folks were "flying on brooms" over their fields.

Eric Butterworth, in his book *The Universe is Calling,* speaks of paganism, as he shares these thoughts, ***"One of the grave mistakes that we make in our study of primitive cultures of the far-distant past, and even now in studying underdeveloped parts of the world, is to refer to the people as pagans. In the early study of religion, the concept of paganism is an unfortunate one. Let's look at this word, understand it, and then make a commitment to eliminate it from our vocabulary. From our Christian or Jewish background, we have used the word pagan to mean nonbeliever, coming from a feeling that "my God" is the "only God," and anyone who believes in any other "god" is stupid – thus a pagan ...***

At best this was unkind, and at worst it was a dangerous root of prejudice and an ethnic slur. Much of this cultural putdown originated with the Christian missionaries who labeled as pagans people in the cultures of Africa, China, India, and the native Indians in America."

Charles Fillmore set forth an interesting premise on paganism and the roots of the Trinity in a talk that he gave on Sunday, January 27, 1929. He stated:

Toni G. Boehm

"This doctrine of the Trinity did not originate in Christianity, as popularly understood. It was introduced into Christianity by an eminent scholar of Carthage, and, like a great deal of our Christian doctrines, it has a pagan origin.

A pagan origin! Could it be that the roots of the Sacred Trinity came from the country dwellers, who created it as part of their worship of the Great Mother, within the context of their feminine-based spirituality?

Fillmore, in *The Revealing Word*, defines pagan from a metaphysical standpoint as *"one in any age who believes in the power of material things."* With this definition in mind, one could say that a pagan is a person who is attached to the things of the world or who is still not fully awake to his or her divinity, because he or she is misplacing his or her source of power. It seems to me that could describe any one of us, and, undoubtedly, early Divine Mother worship did have elements of this in it."

Fillmore goes on to say: *"but, nevertheless, it* [the Trinity, with its pagan roots] *is good, and it was accepted by our Christian fathers because it was true ... The Holy Spirit [the third part of the Trinity] is the manifest side of God. God is Principle ... And the Holy Spirit is the action of God, and when we understand this and look about us for the evidences of spiritual action, we find them on every hand."*

The Holy Spirit and Its Relationship to the Feminine nature of the Divine

In the same talk (mentioned above), Fillmore shifted directions somewhat and moved on to a discussion about the Holy Spirit and Its relationship to the Divine Feminine. This shift in direction fits right in with our premise that a return of the balance in consciousness of humankind can only happen through a return of the Divine Feminine into conscious awareness – and, with that, a full acceptance of the Divine Feminine's role in spirituality and in the world.

Fillmore shares: *"In an analysis of the Holy Spirit, we find that it has been used by religious people in every age, but not fully understood ... The love of God is [the] Holy Spirit. When we understand the real character of Holy Spirit, we will see that it has been and is being worshiped by man everywhere. The Holy Spirit, let us say, is the Divine Feminine of God. We know that God is Wisdom, God is Love. Love is the Holy*

Spirit, or the Divine Feminine and that is the Holy Mother."

This last section leads us to another set of questions: If the Holy Spirit is the feminine nature of the divine, then what impact does leaving the Divine Feminine out as a part of our religious heritage have on the consciousness of humankind? If, as it says in Genesis, we are made in God's image and God is portrayed as only a male figure or image – then in whose image are women made? Where are the feminine role models in religion?

It would seem that men receive incredible validation by an all-powerful, masculine deity role model. This is a very overt message being given to men – albeit, perhaps, being given in a covert way. And if this message of power and "specialness" regarding men is so blatant, then what kind of messages are we sending to women if they have no place in the Trinity, the foundational underpinning of Christian religion?

To answer these questions, let us look at the subtle messages that are given in the creation story. The covert message is threefold. The first is that Eve – the feminine, or woman – was made from a rib of man, with an inference that this is just a very small part of man and that because she was made second, it makes woman secondary to man. After all, God created his favorite first, right?

The second message is that Eve, or woman, is held personally responsible for the "fall of man." Paradise was lost because of the antics of a woman who wouldn't listen to God and who used her feminine wiles to tempt an "innocent" man into committing sinful acts.

The third subtle message that is sent forth as an archetypal communication informs the collective consciousness of humankind that it should be on guard, lest women do this again.

And let us not forget how this story of Eve's plunge into "sinfulness" ends. It culminates in a decree that says women will have to pay forever in order to atone for Eve's actions. To atone for these wanton ways of Eve, women will have to suffer in pain through childbirth and in life. These so-called negative actions of Eve, ultimately, are the condemning factor for all women and for the Feminine nature of the Divine.

This image of Eve, the Feminine nature of the Divine, and of woman as it comes to us from our religious past, holds an image of woman as vamp, siren, temptress, aggressor, enchanter, seductress, troublemaker, dissident, pest, demagogue, and agitator. Does this sound like a role model that anyone would aspire to? Yet on a collective unconscious level, this role

Toni G. Boehm

model is an archetypal pattern that we have subtly accepted as a societal norm for women. And we live this archetypal pattern out consciously and unconsciously, still today.

You say that we do not! Allow me to give you a few examples of how these subtle thoughts are still held in the collective unconscious mind and how they affect women today. There are countries where women are not allowed to own property. Women and their children are considered the property of the husband. Why? Do they believe that a woman is not capable of taking care of property? Is it that the men of the culture feel more validated when everything is their possession and they can do with it what they please? Or perhaps it is because Eve was given charge of a Garden and she didn't do a very good job of taking care of it or of following directions.

Then there is female infanticide. Female babies are being aborted because they are not considered worthy of keeping as their male counterparts. Do not delude yourself that this is not going on today. Could this practice stem from the idea, as feminist Mary Daly says, "**Where God is male, male is God?**" This idea makes men an undisposable commodity. After all, you wouldn't get rid of God, would you?

And let us not forget the (barbaric) practice of female circumcision. Have no doubts – it is still being practiced today in various areas of the world. Why is this done? Because of the fear of a woman's "excessive sexual appetite." The following statement was written by an early church father and philosopher around the fourth century A.D., when they were discussing the role of women in the church. He wrote, **"One chief weapon of the female is pleasure."** Undoubtedly he was influenced by Philo.

One would have to admit that these are very subtle yet real messages that are being sent forth, not to mention that none of the aforementioned ideas are very validating or loving images of women or for the feminine image.

Charles Fillmore made another statement in the previous lesson. He said, **"God as Holy Spirit is doing Her perfect work in us, just to the extent that we recognize it and allow it to do its perfect work."**

The Holy Spirit, the Divine Feminine, is doing Her perfect work, but we do have to recognize Her. The issue is not whether She exists. The issue is that we as a collective society do not recognize Her or consider the attributes She holds, to be of great value.

For example, if you would take a poll and ask people what they admire more – intellect or intuition – the answer would be "intellect and knowledge." Intuition is not an attribute that we generally hold in high esteem. It is something that is usually considered necessary only when you are having your palm read. In fact, the cliche goes, "Oh, that is women's intuition."

Yet intuition was an absolutely imperative aspect of Jesus' ministry, which He reflects over and over again throughout the Gospels. Each time He teaches, heals, or comes in contact with a person in some way or other, He reveals a truth to them that is brought forth through the intuitive faculty.

For example, in John 4, Jesus asks the Samaritan woman to go get her husband. She says that she does not have a husband, and He concurs. In fact, He shares with her that He knows she has had five husbands. But He does it in such a noncondemning and loving way that her heart is opened to the truth of His message. (Jesus, in this situation, utilized intuition, love, and noncondemnation – all feminine-type traits.)

How did Jesus develop or obtain this intuitive, knowing ability, this feminine trait? I believe it happened at the River Jordan when He was being baptized by John the Baptist. Metaphysically, John represents the illumined intellect, the first step in spiritual realization, which prepares the way for the Christ experience. This is the material cleansing of our conscious mind, which redeems us from error thinking through the power of the Word. It is, however, only a beginning step, for John states that there is something more powerful coming, a baptism of fire. (Matthew 3:11: "He will baptize you with the Holy Spirit and with fire." NRSV)

If we return to Fillmore's premise that the Holy Spirit is the Feminine nature of the Divine, then logic would lead us to believe that once one does the initial work, which is the building of a strong spiritual foundation through developing the aspects of the Divine Masculine (for example: one develops the masculine trait of **Strength** to overcome the sense of victimhood; one learns the proper usage of the **Power** of the Word; one develops an understanding of the proper use of **Will**; and so on), then the next type of work one would be ready for would be that of the Feminine nature of the Divine. Therefore then, perhaps in the second baptism, the baptism of the Holy Spirit, Jesus received an initiation into a deeper understanding of the feminine nature of the Divine – an awakening that provided Him with a whole new set of tools, for it is after His baptism of fire that three things occur:

1. He "endures" and walks successfully through the Wilderness experience
2. He overcomes the temptations of the world as the Devil, His personal adversary, attempts to seduce him, to use His "newly found" authority and mastery for power and self-glory in the world.

3. He is then able to call forth His "disciples" (innate powers at a deeper level.) and He begins His ministry of teaching and performing miracles, and healing.

Why and how was He able to do accomplish these things? Because He was then living from a state that reflected a balanced consciousness, a state I call "integrative spirituality." It was from this state of integration and balance that He was prepared to go forth and begin His real ministry and do His deeper work in taking on the fullness of the Christ consciousness.

In a work entitled, *"The Holy Spirit–Its Work In Man: Part II,"* a Sunday lesson given January 27th 1929, Charles Fillmore shares the following;

"Jesus Christ ... reached the limit of his masculine consciousness ... He was the light of the world, the heat of the world ... but He could not express Himself on that plane until He became the Holy Mother, until He was the Mother of us all ... We are joint heirs with Him ...

so we must think about God as Mother as well as Father. We must think about and worship the Holy Mother and talk to the Holy Mother, and enter into that Holy Mother consciousness within us ... We have not that concept of the mother."

The age of Pisces was the John the Baptist stage of consciousness. For more than two thousand years humankind has been developing the masculine traits of God, preparing the way for the descent of the Holy Spirit. Preparing for the next stage of consciousness evolution, to be imbued in consciousness with the traits of the feminine in order that we might go forth, as Jesus did and do our deeper work – a work that will eventually lead to the transfiguration of consciousness, both personally and collectively.

The Feminine Nature of the Divine Reveals Herself in the Book of Revelation

It is time to allow the Holy Spirit, the Divine Feminine, with all the unique and special gifts that She has to bestow upon humankind, to return fully into conscious awareness and to see where She is desiring to lead us.

In the previously mentioned, 1930s work *"The Hidden Man of the Bible,"* there is a article entitled, *"The Hidden Man of the Bible: Divine Feminine."* In it Fillmore, metaphysically and mystically, interprets Rev. 12: 1-6, the passage regarding the pregnant woman clothed with the sun. Eloquently, Fillmore shares his views on where the Divine Feminine is leading us and what it is that She represents in each of us.

"The 12th chapter of Revelation depicts the activity of the Divine Feminine in each soul, when that soul is spiritually quickened, and is raising up out of sense consciousness into the universal or spiritual consciousness. Have you the understanding to perceive the activity of the divine feminine, as you read the chapter, and to behold the directive power of the Lord, every step of the way? It is an out picturing of the spiritual forces working in your soul, in my soul ...

The woman clothed with the sun. Clothed in spiritual light – rays of spiritual light. Arrayed with spiritual understanding. Saturated with spiritual understanding. Some people get spiritual understanding within, but when it comes to getting the outer spiritual understanding, to applying in outer ways, they lose connection ... But here is a picture of the divine feminine within us, struggling to deliver ... the Christ child or positive spiritual consciousness, over which sense consciousness can never rule any more. Travailing with child. Clothed with the sun – the moon under her feet. The moon is the intellect. No longer depending upon the intellectual concept of spirituality – it must work out in soul and body consciousness. The intellect has had its day. Now it is a servant of the spiritual man. The moon is under the feet of the great femininity."

Toni G. Boehm

Exercise:
What Do You Believe?

This is an exercise that I personally have both participated in and facilitated, it always calls forth an interesting response from those participating.

Purpose: To bring to conscious awareness your thoughts about the qualities, strengths, and attributes of God, humankind, man, and woman.
Setting: Chairs arranged in a circle, with soft music playing in the background
Material: Flip chart, markers, paper and pencil, tape, music, and CD player.
Instructions: This exercise will be done in five parts.

Part I   The facilitator asks the group to define how they grew up seeing God by asking these questions:
"What were the beliefs that you held, as a child about the qualities, strengths, biases, and/or attributes of God?" "What did God look like to you?"
(Remind the group that this is not a test. They are to be very honest in their responses.)
All the responses are to be recorded, exactly as spoken, on a flip chart or large piece of paper. When the group has completed their thoughts, tape the paper on a wall in sight of everyone.

Part II   The facilitator asks the group to define how they see or have seen humankind by asking these questions:
"What beliefs do you hold about the qualities and attributes of humankind?"
All the responses are to be recorded, exactly as spoken, on a flip chart or large piece of paper. When the group has completed their thoughts, tape the paper on a wall in sight of everyone.

Part III The facilitator asks the group to describe the beliefs that they hold or have held about the qualities, attributes, and so on of men in general. All the responses are to be recorded, exactly as spoken, on a flip chart or large piece of paper. When the group has completed their thoughts, tape the paper on a wall in sight of everyone.

Part IV The facilitator asks the group to define how they see or have seen women by asking these questions:

"What beliefs do you hold about the qualities, attributes, and so on of women?"

All the responses are to be recorded, exactly as spoken, on a flip chart or large piece of paper. When the group has completed their thoughts, tape the paper on a wall in sight of everyone.

Part V The facilitator has the group silently review the four sheets of paper and then has each person write down what he or she sees while comparing the different groups. Then, a discussion is held.

*Note: *What usually is seen in comparing these four groups is that the attributes assigned to God match the attributes and qualities assigned to men. And the attributes assigned to humankind match the attributes and qualities assigned to women.*

*(Do not discuss this *Note beforehand. Wait for the moment of self-discovery within the group.)

(Exercise Adapted–Source Unknown)

Drawing by Leslie Bradshaw

ᛐ Chapter Three ᛒ

An Unending Quest for Remembrance:
The Feminine Nature of the Divine Returns Through the
New Thought Movement

"Encouraged by my wife,
I persevered when almost at the point of failure ...
Had I been alone I would more than once
have thrown the whole thing over
and gone back to my real estate business."
—Charles Fillmore as quoted by Neal Vahle in
Myrtle Fillmore: Torch-Bearer to Light the Way

If one were to ask, "What has helped create the most dramatic shift in the consciousness of humankind?" I am sure that many would say. "The invention of the printing press" For with the printing press the shackles that had bound the minds of the people began to be dissolved and no longer could organized religion halt the evolutionary progression of inquiring minds through the lack of information.

Many of these inquiring-mind types landed on the shores of America. Throughout the Age of Faith in the 1600s and the Age of Reason in the 1700s, the number of these inquiring- mind types grew but their cry for spiritual growth fell on deaf ears, for organized religion was firmly entrenched in its dogmas and creeds and did not see the need for or care to heed the plea of these people.

The close of the 1700s in America brought about the birth of democracy (1776). Inherent in this idea of democracy was a dedication to the right of freedom for everyone and the humanitarian treatment of all. A shift in consciousness was definitely being felt here, but what was it leading to? This shift was preparing the way for an influx of a new stream of consciousness that was about to make itself known in the Nineteenth century, and that was the energy of the Feminine nature of the Divine, coming through the New Thought movement and being taught by women.

Charles S. Braden (1887-1970), a prolific writer on religion and the roots of the New Thought movement, shares these words about the 1800s in his book, *Spirits in Rebellion*. *"Nineteenth-century America ... was a century of industrial expansion ... the exploitation of vast resources of timber, minerals, and oil ... Great cities grew ... Churches followed wherever frontiersmen went ... Young growing America gave rise to a great variety of new social experiments, and naturally enough to new forms of religion"*

These emerging religions that Braden is referring to include Theosophy, Mesmerism, Christian Science, Homes of Truth, Divine Science, Religious Science, Mormonism, Spiritualism, and New Thought – to name a few.

(I would also add that another very important incident occurred in the mid-nineteenth century that was not mentioned by Braden. It was the Civil War. Why this war was important to the dawning of the New Thought movement and the reemergence of the feminine nature of the Divine will be discussed shortly.)

According to Braden, some of these new religions were given the label of "metaphysical," because they went beyond the literal interpretation of life and reliance on the commonly known religious text, the Bible. (The inquiring-mind types were making their mark!)

Braden says, *"This broad complex of religions is sometimes described by the ... term 'metaphysical,' because its major reliance is not on the physical, but on that which lies beyond the physical."*

There seems to be a general consensus among religious historians that the metaphysical movement was initiated by Phineas Quimby, a healer from Portland. These spiritual movements, with their newly developing streams of "radical" religious eclecticism and consciousness, were ultimately divided into two main avenues of expression: one was Mary Baker Eddy's Christian Science, and the other was the collective umbrella known as the New Thought movement. Braden believes that it was Mary Baker Eddy, the founder of Christian Science, who made this new spiritual movement into a religion.

The New Thought movement was a movement without a formal creed, but with definite underpinning tenets that, when summed up, stood for the idea that practicing the presence of God can be reduced to a mental science based on eternal law. This New Thought movement was nonbiased according to race, color, or gender asked for no allegiance to a specific creed believed in the divinity of humankind, and was different from "old thought" in that it upheld the belief that the real meaning of the spiritual path was the discovery of one's own innate divinity – a divinity which was found by going within and tapping one's inner consciousness, or spirit. And this could be done without the aid of an intercessory.

Braden shares the views of contemporary religious scholars on the commonality that existed amongst the branches of this budding New Thought movement, with *"all agreeing upon the central fact that healing and ... every good is possible through a right relationship with the ultimate power in the Universe, Creative Mind."*

Mary Baker Eddy's religion, Christian Science, had the same foundational tenets as the others, yet added an additional spin, for one of her tenets was the belief in God as a Trinity. This Trinity held within it a feminine-energy principle, it was a Father, Mother, and Son, (Trinity), with the Holy Spirit being the Mother aspect. Eddy taught this doctrine from the pulpit, and it was this tenet that called deeply to Emma Curtis Hopkins. (Hopkins was 28 when she found Christian Science and had a personal healing. She may be considered Mary Baker Eddy's most famous pupil and was a teacher to the Fillmores.)

Mary Baker Eddy, as the head of this newfound religion, was said to be very strict and autocratic with her teachings and very particular about who carried the title practitioner of Christian Science. Gail Harley, in her doctoral dissertation *Emma Curtis Hopkins* (1991 – Florida State University), shares that *"Eddy was a Victorian female in a patriarchal culture. Because of Eddy's persistence, the union of religion with a healing movement allowed women to take health into their own hands, rise above dependence on the male dominated medical establishment, and surmount an orthodox religious system. Hopkins had met the model mentor she needed to inspire her to new heights of accomplishment ... In Eddy's eyes 'women had the right to worship, to act benevolently, to work and to pray.'"*

Eddy was not a feminist but she had at the core of her belief system a strong sense of feminine worthiness and a feminine consciousness. The group that is said to have influenced her feminine beliefs about God was the Shakers. According to Harley, this Mother-Father God concept was thought to have been brought to America by the Shakers.

In Spirits in Rebellion, Barbara Brown Zikmund describes the feminine influence that the Shakers held in a threefold manner as: *"1.) Modification of the male god with a god that is both Father and Mother ... 2.)*

Toni G. Boehm

Replacement of traditional marriage with communal celibacy; 3.) A new system of internal government that had elders and eldresses as leaders in contrast to traditional male leadership."

Emma Curtis Hopkins, too, held the feminine consciousness in high esteem, perhaps even more so than Eddy, for Hopkins was willing to take her beliefs and move them into action through social reform. Hopkins was committed to the upliftment of women and used the idea of the female divinity to empower and promote equality for women in a patriarchal culture and in a patriarchal religion. Hopkins was not a radical feminist or separatist. She was an advocate for feminine consciousness.

Early in her ministry Hopkins wrote a small booklet entitled *The Ministry of the Holy Mother.* In this small but mighty book, Hopkins states that **"God, the maker of worlds, [is] God the Father ... The ministry of God is the Spirit of God, the Mother."** Harley said that Hopkins' focus was to **"work with Christian texts and attempt ... to integrate what she believed to be overlooked principles"** (for example, the feminine nature of God as given through and taught by Jesus Christ).

This concept of equality took root and flourished in her work and in her students. It was said that **"Women now have a divine sanction."** Emma Curtis Hopkins' ministry was one of the first to ordain women as ministers, a concept hitherto not commonly heard of. Hopkins encouraged women in the New Thought movement to seek positions of leadership and authority. Why did this branch of Christian Science, or New Thought, spearheaded by Hopkins catch on so quickly? There are three answers that can be given to this question:

1. The first one takes us back to the time right after the Civil War.

R. R. Ruether and R. S. Keller, in *Women and Religion in America* set forth the premise that after the Civil War there was **"the beginning of a massive effort to win rights for women in politics, in the legal system, in church hierarchies and in professional employment."**

However, I believe that there was also something more metaphysical happening. Let us begin with a question, "Why did the Civil War occur?" The underlying premise was that it was being fought for the right of freedom and equality. Included in this premise was the release from slavery and oppression for the African-American population. Thus, the war took on the appearance of two groups fighting over the freedom of a particular segment of the population and whether or not one person had the right to own another person.

But what if the Civil War was actually an outer expression of that greater stream of consciousness I mentioned earlier, a stream of consciousness which had been waiting in the "ethers" until the time was ripe in the consciousness of humankind, for once the shift in consciousness did begin, it was like a house of cards. All types of movements sprung up after this war, one right after another, each one in its own way calling forth into existence a little more freedom and equality for all persons and groups. With the birth of each of these movements, a little more of the fullness of the tenets that America was founded on came into realization.

The beginning movements included New Thought, temperance, Christian Socialism, early Progressivism, political reform, suffragette, unions, and popular psychology (*"Hypnotism is ... a revolutionary new method that could make race perfection possible"* – Beryl Satter, *Each Mind a Kingdom*) – to list a few. You could even add World War I, World War II, and the Vietnam War as examples of movements that were about freeing the oppressed, because each one had, at its core, one group of people that was trying to subdue the freedom of another group, race, or culture.

In regards to the Civil War, it was less than one hundred years earlier when the founding "fathers" set forth a Constitution for the United States of America that declared freedom and equality for all. Yet some of those same men who signed that paper owned slaves and were part of the oppression – even though they declared in word that freedom was one of their founding principles.

From a metaphysical point of view, it is known that the mind cannot hold two opposing thoughts for too long without some type of reaction (physical or external chaos) occurring. The ultimate result of this incongruency is that it will eventually call forth a chaotic situation from which a person will have to make a choice. The Civil War was the eventual external result of that "incongruent internal" mental battle in the consciousness of humankind.

2. The growth spurt during this time of the mid-to-late 1800s, from the esoteric views of Rudolph Steiner, occurred because there was ushered into consciousness a new angelic energy brought in by Archangel Michael. Steiner thought that Michael brought his sword of truth, power, and a new stream of conscious intelligence in order to affect changes in the consciousness of humankind – if that consciousness were open and receptive.

3. The third answer to the great growth spurt involves Emma Curtis Hopkins and a decision she made to "leave ministry" as she had been

Toni G. Boehm

practicing it. Once her movement was established, Hopkins felt satisfied that it could go on without her daily involvement. Hopkins chose to leave Chicago and move to New York City. In New York she was befriended by the so-called movers and shakers of the various artistic communities and of society. These people were very influential in the "new movements" going on, for example, the temperance, the suffragette, and so on. It is believed that Hopkins moved social activism in the ministry from theory to activity.

According to Vahle, Emma Curtis Hopkins was the teacher whom the Fillmore's received "a significant part of their teachings" from and whom they relied on most as they were in their formative years. Vahle says: *"The Fillmores studied with Hopkins during her most productive years as a teacher ... Kansas City had an active branch of Hopkins' college ... In January 1890 ... Hopkins [came] to Kansas City to teach the primary course ... The Fillmores, who had been active as Christian Science practitioners since 1887 and as publishers of Christian Science materials since 1889, were deeply impressed by Mrs. Hopkins and her teaching ...*

"In June 1980 Hopkins returned to Kansas City ... Students qualified themselves for the Christian Science ministry by taking the course ... The Fillmores completed the advanced course and were ordained as ... ministers in December 1890 ... Many of the teachings of Emma Curtis Hopkins can be found in the work of the Fillmores ... The Fillmores never knew Mary Baker Eddy personally."

It is undoubtedly from these two influences, the teachings of Christian Science as set forth by Mary Baker Eddy and the personal influence and teachings of Emma Curtis Hopkins, that the Fillmores were awakened to the feminine nature of the Divine.

James Dillet Freeman, poet and prolific writer, in the May 1987 issue of *Unity Magazine*, says this about Myrtle Fillmore and the role of women in general in the New Thought movement:

"We should not forget that it was Myrtle Fillmore who first got the idea that became Unity. The couple attended a lecture – probably given by Dr. E. B. Weeks, who had been sent to Kansas City by Emma Curtis Hopkins.

"Charles said the meeting did nothing for him, but when Myrtle walked out of the meeting ... she went home, threw away her medicines, through prayer and meditation demonstrated her healing, and began to teach truth ...

"It is Charles himself who tells us that only after seeing the results his wife obtained, he decided to see if he, too, could contact God and receive help ... The original impetus came from Myrtle ... If you look at the history of the Unity movement, you see how important women have been. From its beginning they have done most of the work at Unity School of Christianity ... This is no less true of other New Thought churches. Johnnie Coleman in Chicago draws thousands of persons every Sunday to her church ... Men have had a role to play in New Thought, but there can be no question it was the women who were the pioneers in its growth."

The Feminine Nature of the Divine's Radical Reemergence in the Twentieth Century

At the turn of the century as we made our way into the 1900s and the last hundred years of the millennium, the various streams of the New Thought movement began to make their mark on the consciousness of humankind. This influence continued, albeit in a subtle manner, throughout the first half of the Twentieth century. The New Thought movement spread and began to call forth new ideas and ideals in the minds of those committed to its teachings.

For the past several thousand years, the world has been steeped in what I like to refer to as "masculine-dominated thought forms." I use the term masculine-dominated thought forms instead of patriarchal thinking, for it feels as if this term is less apt to set up an us vs. them consciousness. In reality, when we are totally honest, whether we are male or female, we all carry and uphold in consciousness these masculine-dominated thought forms and ideals.

These masculine-dominated thought forms – when allowed to take dominance or, perhaps better said, when left without a "partner" to "temper" or counterbalance them – uphold and accept as the norm the following: aggressive behavior, power over those perceived as weaker, success at any cost, the building of large empires, and so on. This behavior is often enacted regardless of the cost to human life or the environment. Included in this concept is the idea that technological advances are based solely on results as determined by the intellect (the masculine), without regard for the inclusion of the feeling nature (the feminine).

Toni G. Boehm

Although the New Thought movement was growing and expanding, the above-mentioned masculine-dominated attributes were deeply rooted in the consciousness of humankind. Thus they were the majority of the types of thoughts that were influencing and affecting day-to-day living for the masses.

However, a change in consciousness was happening, and the effects of this shift would soon be felt, for humankind was progressing onward and upward and insidiously the Feminine nature of the Divine was making Her mark on consciousness.

World War II and advancing technology brought us to the brink of a major decision. Do we use the newly discovered atomic technology, the atomic bomb, to end the war? And if we do, what cost will we pay in the terms of the destruction of human life and the environment? After weighing the pros and cons, the decision was made to drop the bomb.

(Please note that I am not making a judgment as to whether the dropping of the atomic bomb was right or wrong. I am attempting to outline for you, the reader, the events as they historically unfolded and how the reemergence of the Feminine nature of the Divine consciousness was affected along the way.)

I do strongly believe, however, that the dropping of the atomic bomb sent a shiver throughout the "emotional and physical body" of earth, for if the adage that the microcosm is a reflection of the macrocosm and that "as above, so below" is true, then what we do to one affects all – whether it is a person or an earthly body. Technology, which when used for a higher purpose is meant to take us to greater levels of advancement, had then taken us to a place of destruction, and the consciousness of earth and ultimately humankind retorted with a silent cry of "No more!"

A cosmic shudder rippled throughout the physical, mental, emotional, and spiritual bodies of earth and of humankind, and those undulating vibrations left an inaudible but definite message that said, "We can, as a species, no longer go forward in this manner of self-destruction." It was then time to begin to temper and balance the masculine-dominated thought forms.

It took a few years for the fullness of the message to move us into the next phase of evolution, but here is what I believe happened. After this shock to the psyche of the emotional body of earth and of humankind occurred, another set of "movements" was born, including the peace movement, the civil rights movement, the feminist movement, the goddess movement, the environmentalist movement (save the forest and the trees), the Green Peace movement, and more. All these movements came forth to ask humankind several questions: "How are you going to continue living life?" and "Are you ready to consciously incorporate into your awareness a sense of oneness, equality, and connectedness – the attributes of the Feminine nature of the Divine?" or "Will you remain living from a sense of separation and lack of connectedness?" It was a time to begin to make a conscious choice.

The Feminine nature of the Divine was then taking a stronger stand in consciousness. She had found a new footing, through the New Thought movement, and She was asking us, as a collective body, to *wake up* – wake up to all of the ways that we were raping, destroying, abusing, and causing suffering to Her body and to each other. She was ready for us to recognize that She is alive and that She is determined – no demanding – to be heard and felt in every cell of our beings.

In regard to the question I posed at the beginning of this chapter – "What has helped create the most dramatic shift in the consciousness of humankind?" – I personally believe the answer is not the printing press, but that it involves the stream of consciousness which was making itself known in the latter half of the nineteenth century. Flowing in on that stream of consciousness was a new awareness – it was the awareness of the Feminine nature of the Divine – and it was coming in through women in the form of the New Thought movement.

Why do I believe this feminine stream of consciousness to be the bearer of the most dramatic shift in consciousness? All you have to do is look at what has happened since the time "Her" attributes have become anchored in human consciousness. In a period of approximately one hundred years, we have had more advancements for the consciousness of humankind in the context of social, technological, physical, scientific, personal and spiritual changes than we had throughout all of history up to that time. Regardless of appearances to the contrary, the chaos and upset making themselves known in society and in our personal lives, Her influence has been a mighty force for change and for good – in the consciousness of humankind.

Toni G. Boehm

Reweaving the Fabric of HumanConsciousness –
Thread II:
Coming Into an Awareness of the Feminine Nature of the Divine

Thread II, woven throughout Chapters 4 and 5, sets the stage for a deeper understanding of how we as a collective world society have lived from a consciousness that holds masculine-dominated thought forms as our priority. We will explore the personal cost that society has suffered as the result of the repression of the Feminine nature of the Divine aspect of our being and how this has affected us as a race, a society, and a universe.

Wandering the landscapes of Chapter 6 we come into a new level of awareness regarding the work of the Feminine nature of the Divine, one that leads us into a freshness of thought around Her role in our lives. We see how She uses our heart as Her crucible, as She begins to work Her wonders in us, as She teaches us how to live from the wisdom of our hearts. Through this process a new realization is birthed, one that reveals to us that we are indeed sacred humans.

Exploring Chapter 7, we find ideas that take us from soul mates to tantra, this probing calls us to delve into the creative urge of the universe that is inherent with us, our sexuality.

Do not be misled by the personality of the Holy Spirit
and the reference to it as 'he' ... Holy Spirit is the love of Jehovah
taking care of the human family and love is always feminine.
Love is the great harmonizer and healer,
and whoever calls upon God as Holy Spirit ...
is calling upon the divine love."

–Charles Fillmore
Jesus Christ Heals

ᴥ Chapter Four ᴥ

Saying "Yes" to Her Initiatory Fires

"Everything is gestation and then bringing forth ...
Await with deep humility and patience the birth hour of a new clarity."
– Rainer Marie Rilke
Letters to a Young Poet

A glass that is full holds no space for expansion, and traditional religion has been full of itself for centuries. Orthodox religious teachings have not allowed any room for the possibility of amplification of such teachings. The door to "possibility" has been slammed closed and locked tight under the guise of the unchangeable Word. Another way it was sealed shut was when Christianity accepted the idea that only a male God existed. Does it make sense to you that if there are a father and a son in the Trinity, there would not be a mother somewhere in the midst? After all, "as above, so below," is said to be the prototype for the world.

A lop-sided, male-only deity interpretation closes the door on possibility and thus denies the expansion of religious teachings into the fullness of their potential. Ultimately, anything that is denied creates a sense of repression in the consciousness of humankind. This repression eventually creates a wound in the psyche that leads to dysfunctional behavior. This happens both in individuals and in collective society.

The problem is that the dysfunctional behavior exhibited by collective society over the past several millennia has not been recognized for its root cause. If indeed it has been looked at it has been misinterpreted and deemed to be coming from another source. What we have been repressing in consciousness is the idea that a Feminine nature of the Divine exists. The result of this repression is a wounding that can be seen in the behavior of the cultures and society's regard of women as second-class citizens, chattels, and possessions.

An example of an out-picturing of this dysfunctional behavior is that there are today (even as we are in the midst of gender-specific religious reforms) certain religious groups demanding that the orthodox teachings specific to their dogma (this includes Christianity, Judaism, Islam, and so on) remain steeped in the hierarchy and patriarchy of their gender-imposed

Toni G. Boehm

masculine-dominated tradition. This tradition says women are second class and do not deserve, have the ability, or have the right to know God. Several articles that speak in depth of this "submersion into patriarchal ideals" that women worldwide have had to experience and are still experiencing appeared in the TheKansas City Star during June 2000. The first one that I would like to share was published on June 18 and said:

"Of particular concern [to the members of Judaism's Reform Movement of the United States and Canada] was the ... preliminary passage of a bill [in Israel] that would imprison women for seven years for holding religious ceremonies at the Western Wall in Jerusalem. The bill sought to block the Israeli Supreme Court's ruling in favor of a group of Orthodox, Conservative and Reform women, called the Women of the Wall. The decision gave women the right to hold services at the wall, including the wearing of prayer shawls and reading aloud from the Torah scrolls. In ... Orthodox tradition, men and women worship in separate areas at the Western Wall, and only men can hold services, while women worship individually."

The other article came a little earlier in the same week. It shared highlights from the Southern Baptists of America convention. At their yearly convention (in 2000), the Southern Baptists accepted a proclamation that said women could no longer be ordained as ministers within their faith. The women who are currently ordained will not be defrocked, but will be allowed to "die" out through attrition.

This brings up several important questions. If they have been ordaining women, did God give them permission for this change in the first place? Then did God have a change of mind and heart? Whom did God speak his change of plan to?

Or possibly, was it "human thought"which said they could ordain and then "human thought" which said they couldn't? I ask this because the God I know doesn't waver. The God I know is eternal, unchanging, and doesn't make mistakes. This same God would not care if the person carrying Its message was male or female. The only thing that would count would be whether the person carrying the message lived from a sense of a pure heart and pure intentions – intentions that hold only that the good of all be carried out. Yes, that is what my God stands for.

A new dawn of realization is coming forth, and women everywhere are awakening to the idea that they, too, have the ability and the right to speak with God. Women are realizing that when they speak to God and listen for God's answer, contrary to conventional "wisdom," the great Universal Presence desires to and does speak to them also.

Women and men must begin to recognize and speak their truths about the misogyny that remains in the world. Individually and as a collective whole, women (and men) must begin to unite in learning how to support women (and all of humankind) everywhere who are just beginning to make their way out of believing that they are victims of life and of biased societal norms. Through a united consciousness, women and humankind will be ushered into the dawn of a new realization, a realization that knows and accepts everyone as sacred beings.

Christ and the Holy Spirit

The following is a quote by Charles Fillmore that expresses the importance of the role of the Divine Feminine in the process of personal and collective spiritual transformation. It is from an article entitled *The Co-Operation of Christ and Holy Spirit*, written in 1939 and an excerpt from the work, *"The Hidden Man of the Bible"*:

We have yet to see a clear explanation of the relation which Christ bears to the Holy Spirit or Spirit of Truth ... The Spirit of Truth, which the feminine of God alone possesses the power to impart the Spirit-Word to men and quicken the Christ Mind in them and assist them in their growth to the Son of God stature ...

"The Sons of God are [not] miraculously wrought. Man is brought forth through the progressive unfoldment of law and no miracle enters into the creative process, [in other words, Fillmore is saying that humankind evolves through an orderly movement of consciousness, which happens through the collective willingness to awaken to the Truth of our beings]. *It is a development of soul and body and requires both masculine and feminine elements to round it out.* [This statement makes it very clear that Fillmore understood it takes both, the masculine and the feminine, working together to activate the Christ consciousness.] *As the body of the physical man is formed from the combined substances of the father and the mother, with the mother predominating, so the spiritual body* [the regenerated, renewed, and revitalized body of the ascended Christ] *is a transformation of those elements.*

Toni G. Boehm

"We shall never understand the powerful part the Holy Spirit [the feminine nature of the Divine] *plays in the redemptive work of Jesus Christ until woman is given her rightful equality in God-Mind. So long as the masculine God is given all the creating, we shall not realize the softening influence of the Spirit of Truth. Our Bible writers and translators have allowed the temporary dominance of the masculine ... to submerge the finer and more beautiful ideas of the feminine.*

"Although there are many splendid feminine characters in the Bible, they are so submerged by the quantity and boastful quality of the masculine that their creative importance is seldom mentioned. [These last few sentences speak volumes about Fillmore's beliefs around the importance of the work of the Divine Feminine in the regeneration of the body and the taking on of the Christ consciousness.] *... The Holy Spirit has the power to awaken and free the souls of men from their sleep of sense* [their sense of separation from God.] *... Christianity has been personalized and masculinized to death ...* [and] *Woman is failing to measure up to her Divine type because of the picture of her physical origin* [here Fillmore is referring to the creation story that we discussed earlier, and in this allegory, Eve is made from the rib of Adam, which subtly suggests a secondary or lesser position] *which is being carried in the race consciousness* [the collective unconscious mind of humankind].

Chapter Five

The Personal Cost of Repression

*"Trying hard to please women often
sacrifice their feminine nature to carry out
the traditional roles and rules of society."*
— T.G.B.

My family wanted a boy, hence my name Toni. I was named after my father's father. I decided at an early age to be the best girl/boy possible in order that the family might hold me in esteem. Trying hard to please, I unconsciously, sacrificed my feminine nature to carry out the traditional masculine roles of power, aggression, and success. At what cost did I do this? I know now that it cost me the awareness of my image as a whole being and that it cost me a lack of contact with the "deeper" Feminine aspect of my being.

I refer to the way that I was living life as being caught in the trappings of the masculine-dominated thought forms. Notice that although I say masculine-dominated thought forms, this is not about men and women, male and female, or gender. This is about a pattern of thought contained within the normative societal thought forms – thoughts and beliefs which have become entrenched in everyday living, norms which include the traditional roles that we set up for each gender and that we have accepted as normal ways of being. By buying into these thought forms, we have limited the potential of both genders.

We all participate, male and female alike, in holding these masculine-dominated thought forms in consciousness and in holding the unique "specialness" of the male gender. We do this because we have been subtly indoctrinated through our cultural norms of what constitutes correct gender behaviors, attitudes, jobs, and so on.

The current movement (and it is growing) to reclaim the Feminine nature of the Divine and of Self should be celebrated, not feared or dismissed. This is not about women taking over the domain of power, but this is about reweaving the rent that has been made in the fabric of the tapestry of societal consciousness.

By taking the threads that have been unraveling for millennia, we can create a new pattern of consciousness which honors harmony, peace, balance, and other feminine-type qualities. We can weave a new picture that reveals a consciousness and a society where everyone is taught that power is not defined as power over another, but as stated so eloquently by Dr. Carolyn Myss in her book *Anatomy of the Spirit. "power is a manifestation of the life-force ... "* and our work is to learn how to regulate the flow of that life-force so that we are receiving fully of the power of its benefits.

When individuals and society begin to incorporate this truth into the core of their belief systems, then and only then will we have learned what true power and authority mean. Power comes from within, bringing with it a sense of inner peace that goes forth from us to be reflected in our world.

Desiring to study the feminine nature of the Divine and spirituality is not about taking a stand that says, "Men are not good" or 'bad man because of what you have done." It is about making a statement relative to an inner longing that lives in our cellular memories and desires to be remembered. It is a reclaiming of the divine heritage that said, "In our image let us make them, male and female."

Consciousness means awareness, knowing. What we know is that we are all made in the image and likeness of God. If there was only a male God, then who is us and our? This was said in this way in order that we might remember that the two, masculine and feminine, together make and form the one. This knowing creates a sense of wholeness and equality for all of humankind.

Taking the time to study the history of the Feminine nature of the Divine, including the ancient goddess cultures, brings an awareness that there was a time when being born in the female image was honored and exalted. During these times there was not anything that a female could not do or position she could not hold. It was all in the scope of her domain, for the Divine Feminine, or Goddess, image and energy were revered. Women held primary positions and roles within the clans and tribes, for women in these ancient times were governors, judges, priestesses, oracles, poets, queens, and leaders of the people – the same types of positions that up until the past few decades of our lifetime have been traditionally filled by men.

Impotence Changed to Power

Charles Fillmore, in a talk he gave on Mother's Day, May 10, 1925, entitled *"Regeneration: Impotence Changed to Power"* shares his views on women, motherhood, and the importance of calling forth the activity of the Holy Spirit (the Divine Feminine), for both men and women.

"This is Mother's Day. Mrs. Fillmore covered that phase of today's word and perhaps I ought not to add anything to it. But although I believe in mothers, I believe that our mothers should not be held down to what the world calls motherhood, altogether. They should be lifted up into spiritual consciousness.

"As Isaiah says in one of his verses: 'Break forth in song of ye barren, for you shall bring forth as the sands on the sea shores.' Nearly all teachers about mothers tell the mothers how blessed they are and how they should rejoice that they are mothers, and the young girls are told they should prepare for motherhood.

"Is that the highest aim of man, to generate? [Are women only to be thought of as a vehicle for procreation?]

"Jesus Christ when going to the cross and they followed him lamenting and crying out at the death he was to suffer, said: 'Do not wail for me but look out for yourselves, especially you mothers.' He saw that motherhood on the physical plane was not the highest for women. It is not the highest for men.

"We have a spiritual man to develop. Every woman has a soul to save so why should she be busy with saving her soul. 'But,' you say, 'she must be unselfish, give herself up to the race.' We are coming to a higher place and women have the privilege of developing their souls just as well as men. We, in our work [the Unity work] think mothers have all the privileges of man ...

"We are every one of us male and female but is the masculine man developing the Divine [Feminine] in himself? ... Our good mothers [Fillmore seems to be using this as a term referring to women in general], *loving mothers, we want to remain at your knees until we get through with you, then we go off by ourselves and you can go off by yourself. Women should stand side by side with men, if it is in the courts of justice, all right. If it is in the courts of government, all right. That is the bringing forth of the mother, [the Divine Feminine] when that mother is brought forth we will have equity, justice, equal rights between man and woman.*

"We will come to a time when children will be brought forth spirituality.

Greater are those [children] *brought forth spiritually than those brought forth physically.* [Fillmore is alluding to the idea that when couples come together in love, in prayer, and in a conscious awareness that they are participating in the act of cocreating a new life and not just performing an act or an activity of procreation, the baby drawn to these couples will be more spiritually advanced, more consciously aware of their Divinity. Thus these souls will add to the overall advancement of humankind as a spiritual species.]

"We can't suppress women any longer. I have probably thought that women had their place at home but I am changing my mind about this. We might as well make up our minds as fast as possible to the fact that you can't keep women out of the pulpit. You can't suppress them. And when you see the Truth, that the man is the image and likeness of God, and 'male and female created He them,' why should we try to make a distinction?

"Let us celebrate Mother's Day every day. It won't be one day out of the year. Let us give them a square deal and give them [all women] *in every way the same privileges we have* [that men have]. *I praise God that we* [Unity] *are doing it and going to do it in a larger degree in the future."*

Charles Fillmore showers us with words that reveal what a liberal thinker and visionary he was. He displayed this not only in his thoughts about the Holy Spirit as an activity of the Divine Feminine, but also in his thoughts about the role of women in the workplace and in life.

The Earth Is the Womb

The earth is the living womb
of the Feminine aspect of the Divine.
Planted here within
the sacred darkness of Her being,
we gestate and grow.
Over and over, through many lifetimes,
the seeds of the life memories contained
within our souls break open.
Each seed-memory
from the past grants us
the lessons that we have come to cultivate and unfold
as we grow into
the Light of Divine Love,
until at last the final seed
breaks open and we bloom into the full awareness of the
truth of our being.
Our time of gestation
having been completed,
we are ready to leave
the safety of Her womb
and to be birthed as Love beings,
into other realms
beyond this space and time.

— T.G.B.

Toni G. Boehm

Exercise:
Welcome to the World

Purpose: To welcome us to the world, to have each participant remember that he or she is special. To have each person join in remembering that – regardless of the circumstances of his or her birth – he or she was wanted. To have each person remember that in being given the gift of life, he or she has come here (to earth) to add to the consciousness of the collective whole.

Setting: Anywhere you can spread out and form two rows.

Materials: Music and CD player

Instructions: Divide the group into two equal rows. Have them stand across from each other in a straight line, about an arm's length away from each other. When the exercise is about to begin, have them clasp the hands of the person across from them to form a womblike structure that the people will crawl or walk through.

Select two people to start. One person goes to the far end and stands as the midwife, the "welcome to the world" person for those coming through. The other person starts the passage through the canal. One at a time, each person will come through the birthing canal. As the birthee comes through the canal, the people whisper how much she/he is wanted and loved, what attributes she/he is bringing into the world, and other wonderful and kind things.

At the end of the birthing canal – the entrance to the world – the midwife hugs the newly birthed and welcomes her/him into the world with these words:

"Welcome to the world. We have been waiting for you. You are wanted."

Continue till each member of the group has had an experience.

ᴖ Chapter Six ᴖ

Her Gifts and Blessings

"Having forgotten who we are as spiritual beings
has entrenched us in the mire of materiality.
Turning within to the place where Divine Love resides
allows us to begin to remember."

– T.G.B.

In doing research several years ago, I came across the following quotes by Russell, Tomberg, and Steiner, they stirred something within my soul and caused me to ask myself deeper questions, about life and Truth and me.

The first quote comes from Peter Russell and his book *A White Hole in Time*. Russell sets forth the question *"Tomorrow's world will ... be changing even faster. And beyond that yet faster still. But – where are we going? Where will our burgeoning creativity take us next?"* Perhaps the answer to this question lies in the consciousness of humankind and the decisions that we are currently making and going to make as a collective universal society over the next few decades. It would appear that we, the collective whole known as humankind, are now sitting at a crossroads in our evolutionary process and that we are, at the same time, at a point of crisis. The crossroads and the crisis sit at the same juncture of the evolutionary journey.

The crossroads aspect is that we, as a species, are ready to evolve to another level of consciousness, but in that order to take the turn in the direction in which we need to grow, we must have "a new element" introduced into the collective consciousness.

The crisis arises out of the question. Now that we are at the crossroad, are we going to choose to take the path of destruction, which will destroy humankind and all of nature, or are we going to choose to awaken to a new level of awareness? If awakening is the path we choose, then our work as a species is to learn how to make way for and to incorporate this "new element" into consciousness. But what is this "new element" that is trying to birth itself into conscious awareness?

Rudolph Steiner, in his book *Spiritual Hierarchies*, shares the belief that *"it is humanity's great mission to bring freedom into the world, and, along with freedom, what we call, in the purest sense of the word, LOVE. For without freedom, love is impossible ... Freedom and love are two poles that belong together. If love is to enter our cosmos, it can only do so through freedom ... "*

This "new element" that is desiring to birth itself is *love in its purest sense.* In other words, according to Fillmore's definition, it is the Divine in Its feminine aspect, which is God in Its pure and unconditional aspect of love. This divine love can only be brought into conscious awareness as we are willing to surrender our adverse ego (our unspiritualized self) unto the greater power and wisdom of the Divine. If we do not evoke this attitude of surrender, we remain caught in the ego's web of separation and duality, being stuck in the head and the lower heart of human emotions.

The siren song of the last decade has been one of learning to live from the heart. I do not necessarily believe, however, that living from the heart, alone, is the most important thing we must do. That which is most imperative now is the joining of the head and heart. If the head represents intellectual knowledge and the heart represents intuitive knowing, then imagine what can happen when the two come together. With the head and the heart acting from a sense of surrender to the universal will and in alignment with a higher truth that is participating in a state of harmonious interchange, imagine what we will be able to create and attain. All we need to do is begin to surrender our gift of free will and begin to choose to live from this higher state of awareness.

From Valentin Tomberg's work entitled *Meditations on the Tarot* comes the idea that, *"The exoteric church of Peter [the intellect] will make way for the "esoteric" church of John [the heart], which will be that of perfect freedom."* This perfect freedom that both Steiner and Tomberg refer to is the freedom to choose to surrender our free will back unto the Divine and to consciously choose love to be the force and power at work in our lives. This will allow the fullness of the Divine to live consciously in the minds of all of humankind.

It has been said that this "esoteric church" will not be built on a piece of land, but that it will be *"built in the interior depths of our heart,"* for it is through the heart that we touch the pure essence of the unconditional love of the Feminine nature of the Divine and receive Its gifts of intuitive knowing and an unending stream of grace. But we can only build this new church in consciousness as we willingly surrender our heads and hearts unto greater service to the One.

The feminine qualities of the heart (our higher emotional, intuitive, and creative aspects) balanced with the masculine qualities (our intelligent, logical, rational, analytical aspects) will call forth a centered, peace-filled existence within and without. This union will bring about an end to the internal struggle that has existed in our consciousness and that has ultimately revealed itself in the manifestation of our everyday lives and problems.

This does not mean we will be free from problems, but our method of coping will take on a new form, for through surrendering to this union, we will live from a higher state of awareness right here in the midst of our humanness. The union has the ability to create an alchemical process of spiritual transformation that will ultimately call forth the living stream of energy of the "Gnosis-Cardia," the greater wisdom of the heart.

It is this Heart-Wisdom that will bring the purest sense of divine love into matter, into human form. This descent of the Feminine nature of the Divine, or Love, into matter (into our earthen vessels) will form the true "esoteric church." It has also been said that this esoteric church will be a church of the heart, built through the sacred union of the head and the heart, the masculine and the feminine joined as One – Spirit and matter bound in Oneness.

Integrative Spirituality

The head brought into the heart will make the conscious decision to call forth the next phase of being, Love, with the Feminine being brought into union with the Masculine. Then we will experience integrative spirituality. Spirit integrated in Its highest state into every level of our being in this human form.

Each of us, male and female alike, have a feminine phase of being. But as a society we have lost or pushed aside the feminine's values in favor of masculine attributes. We have forsaken the feminine qualities of unity and compassion in order that we might take on the masculine attributes of will, strength, judgement, ownership, might and power — masculine attributes and attitudes which are very important but which have become misdirected and misguided because, on an unconscious level, one half of us has been denied and repressed. And whatever is repressed will find a way to express itself, in some manner – usually with a negative bent.

Toni G. Boehm

We have indeed realized this on some level and have gone in search of "Her," but we have been looking in all the wrong places. This intense pursuit for our feminine (in all the wrong places), has led us to live our lives in what I call the "void of forgetfulness." This "void of forgetfulness" is a state of feeling empty, like an unquenchable thirst. We continually try to fill this empty feeling with things – toys; drugs; booze; money; sex; and this, that, and the other. But somehow the thirst is never satisfied.

Once we begin to remember that the "void of forgetfulness" can never be filled or satisfied with things outside ourselves we begin the journey back to Self which leads to the truth of our knowing who we are as spiritual beings. We start to realize that the "void of forgetfulness" is in actuality, a deep longing to return to Divine Love. It is through the discovery of this spark of Divine Love that we are ultimately led to a state of wholeness, balance, and oneness, and to the integration of the inner masculine and feminine.

And that, my friend, is the answer to the question that Peter Russell asks: ***"Where we are going so fast?"*** We are heading toward a marriage, a union in consciousness of the masculine and the feminine. This union, was known to ancient Greeks as the *hieros gamos*, the sacred marriage. The ancient wise ones understood that in the process of uniting the masculine and feminine aspects which reside within, we will discover the essence of who we are. And if we do not have this discovery, there is a great chance that we will, individually and as a collective consciousness, destroy ourselves.

It is time to say "YES" – to begin to develop in consciousness that "new element" which will take us to the next level of spirituality, integrative spirituality. Vladimir Soloviev, the Russian Eastern Orthodox teacher of Sophiology speaks of this unity, or integration. He states that ***"the principle of ... unity of grace and truth ... is eventually to become the very essence of the life of each individual believer."***

"Man's Feminine Unfoldment"

Charles Fillmore, mystic and cofounder of Unity School of Christianity, wrote, in the July 1936 issue of *Unity Magazine*, an article entitled *"Man's Feminine Unfoldment."* His moving passages reflects how the feminine principle of the soul begins to express itself in humankind, and how it must express itself in order that we might birth ourselves into the next level of conscious awareness:

"The conception and birth of Jesus, as recorded by Luke, conceals and, to the spiritually wise, <u>reveals a soul principle that will save man from death</u> [a revelation that will teach us the secret of regeneration].

"That principle, represented by Mary [Jesus' mother] *is Love. Up to the time of Jesus the feminine principle of the soul, love never had a chance to express itself because of the arrogant dominance of the intellect* [the masculine aspect of being].

"Jesus enthroned woman, [He brought into His conscious awareness and incorporated into His being the energy of the Feminine nature of the Divine. He released the repressed energy of the attributes of the Feminine nature of the Divine that had been held in bondage in race consciousness.]

"[Jesus] *recognized her equality with man* [He recognized the need for the two, the masculine and feminine, to be One], *and she* [the Feminine nature of the Divine] *has since that time been gradually escaping from the age-long slavery of the ...* [race consciousness] *mind.*

"Jesus would have utterly failed in the resurrection of His body after the Crucifixion, if He had not developed the restorative power of Divine love [the Divine Feminine]. *So no man can hope to escape death until he frees the imprisoned love of his soul* [until he or she awakens to his or her Feminine nature]...

"Fear, anger, anxiety and hate paralyze the hearts of men [which is the result of the lack of Divine Love being alive within one's being]. *Like reckless automobile drivers, men crash their hearts and wreck their bodies, and no law restrains them.*

"There is a law and a remedy for this insane destruction of life, and that is Divine love.

"But men are slow to recognize the transforming power of love [people are slow to recognize the transfiguring power of the Feminine nature of the Divine]. *Even Jesus was loath* [at first] *to admit the feminine had any part in His demonstrations. When His mother* [the Feminine nature of the Divine represented as Divine Love] *called His attention to the lack of wine* [to the lack of vital life – he had performed no miracles up till then], *He replied, 'Woman, what have I to do with thee?'* [Jn. 2:4 KJV]

[Jesus is asking what the Feminine nature of the Divine has to do with Him, He goes on to say, "My time has not come." Jesus, from a

Toni G. Boehm

personal, human sense did not believe that He was ready to go forth and perform any great works. Why? Because He had not yet fully comprehended the importance of the Feminine nature of the Divine, of Divine Love, in the miracle-working aspect of regeneration and transformation.

Mary, representing Divine Love in the soul, the feminine aspect of being, saw what was happening in Jesus. She saw that He doubted his ability and that this fear was creating a "lack of vital life" in Him. She was imploring Him to step out on faith, to look past appearance, to look past His fears and to call forth the power of Divine Love into His conscious awareness. He accepted! He turned the water – of the lower emotions of fear, self-doubt, and uncertainty – into wine – He embodied the vital life of God through the regenerative aspect of Love. Through this merger with Divine Love, He was able to realize His full potential and go forth to fulfill His sacred destiny. After all, it was a wedding feast, a time to celebrate the sacred union, the union of the masculine and feminine, the hieros gamos – within Himself. His time had come, Divine Love within Him knew it, His intuitive nature knew it, and He was pushed forward to meet His destiny.]

"But there is a golden thread of love running through all His life, and those who have eyes see that He developed both the passive and the active phases of love ... This [Love] *also represents the beginning in man or woman of that transformation know as regeneration."*

Fillmore shifts thoughts here just a little and moves into what I believe is a great esoteric teaching and a great clue about regeneration: *"We see not only a transformation of the soul, Mary* [after she says yes to the angel Gabriel, she begins her song of praise], *but also the birth in her of a new body of consciousness* [Jesus, the fruit of her womb, contains the sacred elements that she has held in consciousness, which are forgiveness, compassion, humility, meekness, peace, and embracing love], *which develops within the soul as the child is conceived and develops in the body of woman* [like attracts like].

"Thus, Jesus represents the new spiritual body being formed in man from the elements of the physical body [this statement is extremely important–Fillmore is saying that he recognizes that the human body is the vehicle to the spiritual body – therefore, we lift up this body]...

"Mary's exaltation and praise is a vital factor ["My soul doth

Magnify the Lord"] [In the development of the ideal man, Christ Jesus, gratitude in the form of praise appears to be the elementary factor in the regeneration of the body.] *Mary* [Divine Love alive in the soul] *is the central factor in the manifestation of the elemental body out of which the spiritual body is developed.* [it is only through integrating the Divine Feminine into our being that we can birth the fullness of the Christ consciousness, or our higher power]...

"*The popular presentation of Christianity does not give sufficient prominence to the feminine qualities of the soul, represented by Mary the mother of Jesus* [this is a very important statement].

"*All sciences, philosophies, and religions reveal man to be both masculine and feminine in soul quality, and essentially androgynous in body. Jesus developed the feminine qualities* [qualities of love, kindness, tenderness, mercy, patience, and forgiveness – implanted in him through his mother], *and thus demonstrated the Divine feminine in man.*

"*Divine insight reveals this feminine unfoldment to be essential in the regenerated man or woman.* [This may be one of the greatest sentences Fillmore ever wrote for it shows his deep insight into the mystery of eternal life. It is the core teaching that we must get for it is the clue to the taking on of the Christ consciousness. Regeneration is not possible, at the deepest cellular level of our being unless we fully embrace the Divine Feminine, which is Divine Love. Regeneration is the living presence of the masculine and feminine principles of God, united within us, working in us in balance. Through this state of balance, the hieros gamos, the unified force field of the Father-Mother God, we come to know and experience the full power of the Christ consciousness.]

"*The mother principle must be equal with the father principle in being, hence God must be masculine and feminine in Spirit. Spirit is mind, and mind is ideas, hence the masculine and feminine in being must be ideas representing those attributes. When we speak of God as love, we are addressing our Mother-God. God as substance places us in the arms of our all-providing Mother-God. God as wisdom calls forth the Father-God. Thus Divine insight shows us that to gain the mastery, we must understand and invoke the powers of* [Divine] *Mind and Spirit.*" [therefore, in order to be whole, complete, fully realized and at one with the One, we must awaken, engender, and embody the powers of both the Divine Masculine and the Divine Feminine within our beings].

Toni G. Boehm

leslie Bradshaw

ᠵ Chapter Seven ᠵ

The Feminine Nature of the Divine and Sacred Sexuality

> *"**Sensuality** (n.) The quality or state of being sensual.*
> ***Sensual** (adj.) Suggesting sexuality ... sensory.*
> ***Sensuous** (adj.) of pertaining to, or derived from the senses.*
> *Having qualities that appeal to the senses.*
> *Highly appreciative of the pleasures of sensation ...*
> *Sensuous can refer to any of the senses but more often applies*
> *to those involved in aesthetic enjoyment of art, music, nature,*
> *and the like."*
> – The American Heritage Dictionary of the English Language

From the Latin <u>sensibilis</u> and <u>sensus</u> came the words *sensual, sensuous, sensuousness, sensuality, sensualism, sense, sensible,* and *sensitive* to name a few of their derivatives. These words journeyed through Old French and Middle English making their way to contemporary Modern English. Yet it seems that with each downloading of these words into another language came a bleaker interpretation of what the words meant. In the world's interpretation of the word, a fairly negative connotation has been given to the idea of sensuous and sensuality.

According to the dictionary, the word sensuous means "of, pertaining to or derived from the senses." The senses we know as the ability to touch, taste, hear, smell, and see. Can you imagine what a dull world it would be if we didn't have our sense perceptions and pleasures? Our true work, however, is to understand the role of the senses (that is, sensuality, sensation, sexuality, and the act of generation) and learn to use each of them wisely – allowing them to serve us, instead of our using them.

One of the roles of the Feminine nature of the Divine is to help us awaken and remember who we are as sensing and sensual beings – without all the guilt, fear, or shame that has clouded this life center for so long. Let me be very clear here. Being sensual and/or expressing our sensuality sexually is not wrong! It is a sacred part of who we are as human beings. The grand design for human-hood called for the senses, sensuality, and sexuality to be an aspect of our humanness, to be inherent in our make-up. The force of the Divine Feminine as the nature of humankind in its sexual, sensual

Toni G. Boehm

aspect is a power to be reckoned with. No wonder people have become afraid of Her, for they do not understand Her.

With Freedom Comes Responsibility

Does this mean that we can live life without morals or standards? NO! For inherent in awakening to the sense of who we are as spiritual beings comes a renewed sense of spiritual responsibility. There is an old saying that depicts this sense of spiritual responsibility. It states:

"With freedom comes responsibility."

Following along this same line of freedom and responsibility, allow me to set forth a theory regarding the sexual act and its effect on us at a cellular level. Barbara Ann Brennan, in her book *Hands of Light*, speaks of invisible "cords of energy" that connect us physically, mentally and spiritually to other human beings. She believes we create these cords of energy with all persons with whom we develop relationships. The more intimate the relationship, the stronger the energetic cord. It is possible that these cords become so strong that we carry them from lifetime to lifetime.

If there are these invisible cords of energy that form between us when we are in a social relationship, imagine how much stronger and deeper these cords of energy may be between two persons involved in a sexual alliance, be it a one-night stand or a long-standing relationship.

If this is at all true, then it would certainly make sense from a spiritual point of view to be very responsible regarding from whom one takes deposits into his/her system. After all, who wants someone else's *karma*, even if it is only remnants?

If sexuality is a part of the grand design for humankind and we inherently know how to use our sexuality responsibly, what has happened to create such chaos around sexuality and sensuality? How did sensuality or sexuality come to have such a bad name?

For too long now, humankind, through religion, has been seduced into worshiping a transcendent God – a God that takes us out of the realm of earth and out of the realm of our bodies. This separation from the body has set up false beliefs about sexuality and its purpose in the expression within humankind. The word *Mother* in Latin is *mater*, the root of the word *matter*. The Mother is matter; it is Her domain. The Feminine nature of the Divine is the rich, ripe, fecund Mother, pregnant with possibility and creative ideas that are waiting to be birthed through each of us.

A Sense of Disdain for the Body

Humanity has been psychically ravaged by the sense of disdain for the body. It has kept us from fully enjoying and expressing a natural phenomenon of life. This expression is meant to be natural and it is meant to be holy. It is a "both/and" situation, not an "either/or" situation. Bringing the Divine Feminine back into expression will call forth a change a heart, a change of mind, and a new wisdom regarding the body temple. Fillmore speaks of this when he says:

"The Divine Feminine must be brought into expression ... There must be an equalization, an adjustment, a righteousness between men and women in all affairs."

Sexuality, sex, sexual practices, gender-specific relationships, and the concept of soul mates have long been topics of discussions. Previous to the sexual-freedom revolutions of the 1960s and '70s (and television's open discussion and display of sexuality), these discussion where held in private conversations behind closed doors. But that has all changed. As the ad says, "We have come a long way, baby." Or have we?

Sexuality is who we are as a specific gender, male or female. Sex is the act of procreation, pleasure, or duty – take your pick. It has been said of sex that "we can't live with it, and we can't live without it." We know for a fact that the sexual act has been around since the beginning of time; however, during that time it has been twisted, distorted, demeaned, made unholy, trivialized, fantasied over, considered in vogue, considered out of vogue, glorified, exploited, and used and abused in countless other ways.

I would like to share in the next few pages several ideas on the theme of sacred sexuality, and to explore our gender-biased beginnings and their metaphysics through myth.

Soul Mates

Many years ago I read a story whose origin was attributed to Plato (427-347 B.C.E.). It is a myth that describes the experience of how humankind came into being in these male and female bodies and how this experience created the inner urge to find our right and perfect partner, physical complement and soul mate. This is my version of the myth, which does differ, somewhat from the original.

In the beginning of time, the beings that lived weren't human beings as we know them. They were beings that lived in a state of total perfection – containing both masculine and feminine aspects – they were known as androgynes. Each being was complete in and of itself, loving and honoring itself and knowing that it was a pure reflection of the Great One.

During a cosmic council meeting, an elder asked the Great One if It would be willing to put Its androgyne progine to a test, to allow them to be part of an experiment. In this experiment, each being would be put into a state of sleep, then assigned a dominant gender. The other gender or aspect within them would be covered up, but not taken way.

The gist of the experiment was to see what would happen, would this newly formed being with an assigned dominant gender ever rediscover its original state of wholeness? And if it did, where would it begin to look for it?

The new Being would be either a dominant masculine self or a dominant feminine self, yet it would have within it the fullness of the other gender. Once it awoke, however, it wouldn't remember any of these facts. Shortly after the beings were assigned their dominant gender they were sent to a new world.

What happened over time was that the experiment was found not to be successful, for each new being, instead of remembering their wholeness, became mesmerized with their self. The beings took on a personal countenance and personality and began to believe that they were what they appeared to be in their gender-specific clothing. Also, they lost their sense of connection to each other; they felt separate from each other and all things, even the Great One.

It has been said, that it was from this experiment that humankind came into being and that we now go forth unconsciously seeking to recapture that sense of wholeness that we knew in the beginning.

However, our quest for wholeness has us searching outside ourselves. We go about searching for another to fulfill the "empty" feeling that we have inside and to fill our sense of lack and inadequacy which comes from not remembering in whose image we were made.

Having been mesmerized, by our senses and the sensations of the world, into believing that this material existence is the determining factor of our fate, we scour the world searching, high and low, for what we have forgotten—our wholeness. As it says in Genesis 1: 26-27, "Let us make humankind in our image ... male and female he created them." and so far we have, as a collective whole, not remembered that we are complete. We have not remembered, for we have not looked for our wholeness where it really counts. We have not looked within.

The moral of this myth is that we are on a quest to return to knowing ourselves as the one – masculine and feminine. However, in trying to find that wholeness, we go looking for it in all the wrong places and in the strangest of ways, for few ever think to look within.

Generative Life

Stephan A. Hoeller, in his book, *"Jung and the Lost Gospels,"* reports that in the canonical Gospels there are references to Jesus being portrayed as human and "sensuous" in nature. For instance in Matthew 11:19, it states, *"the son of man came eating and drinking, and they say, 'behold a glutton and a drunkard, a friend of tax collectors and sinners.'" In John 4: 27, we find that, "they [the disciples] marveled that he was talking with a woman." In Mark 15: 40, "There were also women looking on from afar ... and also many other women who came up with him to Jerusalem."*

I end with scripture from the Gnostic Gospel of Phillip, found in the Nag Hammadi Library (discovered in the mid 1940's), *"Jesus loved Mary Magdalene more than all the disciples and used to kiss her often ... The rest of the disciples said to him, 'Why do you love her more than all of us?'"* All of these references lead one to think about the fact that perhaps Jesus did have a human appeal and appetite, a magnetism that attracted others and a sensuousness that he exhibited in front of others.

Charles Fillmore, in the book, *The Twelve Powers of Man*, has a chapter entitled *"Generative Life."* In this chapter he discusses his thoughts on sexuality, sensation, generation, and the idea of delving deeper into the mystery of being:

"The Law of generation is undoubtedly the mystery of mysteries in human consciousness ... In the phenomenal world, life is the energy that propels all forms to action ... Life is not in itself intelligent – it requires the directive power of an entity that knows when and how to apply its force. The engineer of the life-force in the body of man [humankind] is the life ego ... It [the life ego or adverse ego] is an animal force ... It

presides over the life and generative function of the body, and because of its tendency to separate and segregate itself from the other bodily functions, it is called the 'adversary.' It is not essentially evil ... but ... its tendency is to centralize all action around its consciousness [its tendency is to keep us focused on our perceived "needs," as determined by thoughts and sensations that have not been lifted up or regenerated by Divine Love]...

"*In order to give man a body having life in itself, God had to endow him with a focal life center located in the generative organs. This center of activity in the organism is also the seat of sensation which is also the most subtle and enticing of all factors that enter into being. But these qualities (sensation and generation) were necessary to man's character, and without them he would not have been the complete representative, or image and likeness, of God.*

"*What metaphysicians most need is a comprehension of the factors that go to make up consciousness. This requires discrimination, judgement and self-analysis ... We must learn to watch our consciousness, its impulses and desires ... Man forms his own consciousness from the elements of God, and he alone is responsible for the results ...*

"*Consciousness* [consisting of the superconscious, subconscious and conscious minds] *is a deep subject ... Concisely stated, three great factors enter into every consciousness – intelligence, life, substance. The harmonious combination of these requires the most careful attention of the ego* [personality or conscious mind], *because it is here that all the discords of existence arise ...*

"*The greatest danger of perversion* [abuse, misuse, or misapplication of the life center] *lies in the direction of the carnal* [meaning nondivinized human thought] *thought of sex ... polluted by ignorance [lack of the proper use of divine intelligence] ... lust has robbed the bodies of the whole race* [lust is sensation not under the control or domain of divine intelligence] *...*

"*Man [each person] is male and female, which are qualities of mind – love and wisdom. Every attempt to lower these divine attributes to the physical must meet with disaster ...*

"*The marriage mystically spoken of in Scripture, and in other sacred books, takes place in the consciousness; it is a soul communion of the two-in-one, more sweet than that between the most harmoniously mated man and woman. This eliminates sex in outer manifestation* [I believe the word sex here is alluding to the idea of participating in a sexual act, for and with anyone, anywhere, just because it "feels" good; this would not preclude engaging in a more mystical form of sacred energetic exchange based on and in divine love, as Fillmore's additional statements indicate] ...

"Do not kill out the life manifesting through your body by denying it away entirely; deny away the sense of impurity with which the animal ego has clothed it ...

"To desire to be instructed by God is the first step in exalting the inner life force."

The bottom line of this discourse is that Fillmore is calling for a sense of responsibility towards the sexual or generative aspect of life, and this sense of responsibility comes when we call upon God for clarity of thought, wisdom, and insight regarding the true function of the life-center. Fillmore is clear and adamant about the role and importance of this life faculty and how we, humankind, have to take a position of responsible action. It is our spiritual responsibility to place our generative/life center under the influence of divine intelligence and wisdom. (Keep in mind that Fillmore was writing during a period when the discussion of the topic of sex and sexuality was not necessarily dinner table discussion.)

I feel it would be remiss not to share a few words about an ancient sexual practice known as *tantra*. Tantric sexuality is a vein of spiritual practice that comes from the Buddhist and Hindu traditions. Three different dictionaries define *tantra* in a similar tone. They refer to *tantra* as a Sanskrit word that means loom (as in weaving), the warp (of a fabric), a ceremony, or a doctrine. They also add that tantra is based on a religious treatise that teaches magical and mystical formulas for worship and attainment of super-human power.

Andre Van Lysebeth, in his book, *Tantra: The Cult of the Feminine* states: *"Tantra also means a 'loom' or 'weaving' which would seem to bear no relation with any form of doctrine. But Tantra perceives the universe as a fabric where everything is interrelated, interconnected, where everything impacts on everything else. If you add the instrumentality suffix tra to the radical tan (to stretch, to spread, to expand), you get tan-tra, literally, the instrument to expand the field of ordinary consciousness in order to reach supra consciousness, the root of one's being and the well-*

spring of unknown powers that Tantra seeks to awaken and harness. Consciousness is not just for the mind – it permeates the physical body, too. The body is not a carcass, a burden, an obstacle to spiritual life; spirituality exists at each and every level of your body ... Flesh and Spirit do not oppose each other."

Tantric Sexuality

In recent years tantric sexuality has become a very popular topic, with seminars cropping up all over. Some of these are taught by genuine masters, while others are being taught by those who have not done their deeper spiritual work and are not living a pure spiritual life, as many recent "religious scandals" have shown.

Tantra as a movement in consciousness is meant to be mystical in its deeper meaning. That might lead one to believe that perhaps it is not at all about the outer act of sexual practice, with all of its positions and configurations, but that perhaps it is an outer symbol of an inner process which takes place in consciousness between the masculine and feminine aspects of being.

We in Western society are like the beings in Plato's story, for we have forgotten our true nature. The deeper mystical meaning of the tantric experience is not about sexual exploitation, but is an experience that takes a combined effort from all levels of being: the physical, mental, emotional, sexual, and more, which most of us have not prepared or trained for properly. Westerners, as Fillmore says, tend to "dissipate the life force" energy through riotous living and recreational sex. The Feminine nature of the Divine comes to teach us that the body and its sensations can and are meant to be enjoyed, yet are called to take us to a higher level.

I believe, on my deepest level, that the ancient teachers who set forth the tantric-type teaching were esoterics. *Esoteric* means "hidden wisdom;" therefore, these ancient teachers who did not have an adequate way to express in words the extreme ecstasy they experienced in a state of total union and bliss with the One, used the closest thing available to them to express the feeling nature of this sacred experience. And that was the body's orgasmic response from a love making experience. They knew that those "who knew" would understand the hidden message and meaning behind the symbology of the pictures and that those who didn't – well, it wouldn't matter anyway, because they weren't ready for a deeper teaching yet.

Tantra, at its deep level, is *"the act of continuous creation expressed by patterns of sexual activity,"* infused with a sense of totally transcendent love. Tantra is the receptive, feminine principle accepting the infusion of the projective, masculine seed, so that together they can create new beginnings, new life, and new levels of existence. Working in tandem, they – the masculine and feminine aspects of being – are the creative process calling forth manifestation.

Relationship in the material world includes a sexual component, of which one facet is the ability to divinize the sexual experience and use it to create the opportunity for an advanced soul to come into manifestation. Divine relationship between two people, in its most sacred form, is two people coming together, being open to one another on all levels of being: mental , physical, emotional, and spiritual. Two people sharing with one another on this level can be a creative and fruitful force for the uplift of humanity.

In sharing his thoughts about the sacred union of two souls, Fillmore is revealing the hidden meaning in tantra:

"When you see the union of soul with soul – when you see that inner marriage which exists between two people that are in harmony you realize the great Truth that there never was a man nor a woman but what there was somewhere the complement; there was somewhere that other soul that when these two were joined in spirit everything moves in Divine Order"

Charles and Myrtle Fillmore gave birth not only to three children in their marriage but also to a new consciousness that grew into a worldwide movement known as Unity School of Christianity. They were united in oneness on the levels of mind, emotion, body (physical), and spiritual. Please be reminded that being united on the physical level of being is referring to a deeper cellular connection, which can mean that two people can live together with or with out physical or sexual contact.

There are several questions that arise out of the thoughts of the last few paragraphs. They include these: Does a person need a partner for the mystical tantric experience to occur? Can a single person choosing not to be sexually active (with partners) or perhaps even choosing to be celibate still achieve this level of creative ecstasy?

The answer is "Yes!" This is because tantra, when rightly understood, is the willingness to go within and allow (the weaving) the melding and mingling of the inner masculine and feminine forces to interpenetrate the whole being on all levels – this is what creates the tantric experience of ecstasy.

This conjugation of the two energies infuses the being with a sensation of divine love that permeates and perfumes every cell and every level of being. In this state a person is a living, creative force, connected directly to the Higher Power. This creative energy flows like juice flowing from a ripe peach, creating sensations and generating a field of life-force energy that initiates us into a more profound sense of the genesis of life, love, and truth.

Looking at tantra as a one-person experience, what if the mystics who first wrote or spoke about tantra had their tantric experiences alone, but in order to put the experience and the emotions into some form of language that tried to express the inexpressible, they chose to use a descriptive framework the masses could relate to? So, feeling at a loss to describe their rapture and ecstasy these mystics elected to describe their experiences with their inner beloved through the erotic imagery of the act of sexual intercourse.

If this scenario just proposed were true, then tantra, as it is has been touted by the common masses and untrained teachers, would not be about sexual physical contact to reach the heights of ecstasy, but would be about sacred sexuality in its purest sense – which is a deeper movement of energy exchanged at the cellular and etheric levels – without a partner! Yet we will always leave room for the idea that the experience can also occur in its purity with a partner!

In Search Of Union

Mating lizards on my back porch,
basking in the sun, then frolicking to and fro.
She runs and he pursues
until at last she stops
and they join together in union, in oneness.
Bodies entwined,
moving to the rhythmic flow
of the eternal dance of the universe,
calling forth the essence of
new life in the process.
How much they remind me of myself and my pursuit
of Oneness with Spirit.
Except it is I who run to and fro
and it is Spirit that pursues,
ever calling,
"Here I am, let me catch you. I am what you desire."
Finally I surrender my will and stand still,
allowing the Sacred Energy to penetrate my being ...
and to fill me
with the essence of new life.

– T.G.B.

Toni G. Boehm

Reweaving the Fabric of Human Consciousness –
Thread III:
The Divine Feminine's "Soul-u-tion" for Humankind

In Thread III, Chapters 8 and 9 call forth the question "What happens when the Feminine nature of the Divine begins Her 'burning' work and we are thrown into the 'fires of transformation'?" Hopefully, what the reader will find is that their questioning will lead to awarenesses, and from there to awakenings and from there to an urge for more questioning. And, all of these working together will lead to the ultimate restoration of the Feminine nature of their being.

The Feminine nature of the Divine is the regenerative nature of God that calls forth from within us the abundant life inherent within the confines of our cellular structure. Thus we come to realize that the human conditions occurring around us are actually wake-up calls which are desiring to take us to the next level of conscious awareness.

Thread III ends with three streams of thought. The first is my summary of the movement of Feminine nature of the Divine in the consciousness of humankind over 30,000 years. The second and third streams of thought are from Andrew Harvey and me. We each share our suggestions that when followed will help reclaim the Divine Feminine for humankind.

When personality is hurt to the death
and surrenders all,
love pours her balm over every wound
and the substance of her sympathy
infuses hope and faith to the discouraged soul."
— Charles Fillmore

ᨳ Chapter Eight ᨳ

Traversing the Dark Night of the Soul:
Sacred Darkness Brings Rebirth

*"Transformation is only possible when
what is to be transformed
enters wholly into the Feminine Principle
of dying and return."*
– Joan Chamberlain Engelsman
The Feminine Dimension of the Divine

I have come to learn that She (the Feminine nature of the Divine) is relentless when She decides that it is time to teach you a lesson. She will take you by the hand and lead you into the sacred darkness of her initiatory playground, the subconscious mind. Here, while embracing you tenderly, She will, in a way that will feel ferocious, ask you to face your shadows and your greatest fears. You always have a choice: you can ignore Her invitation for growth, or you can fully participate. If you say "Yes," She will expect your full participation, and you cannot play games with Her, for the Mother is all-knowing.

Several years ago, what appeared to be a very painful and devastating life experience was, in reality, the Feminine nature of the Divine within me, knocking at the door of my heart – knocking and asking if I was ready to make even more room for Her to live within the spaces of my cellular structure.

It was late August of 1995 when the pain began. Excruciating pain would come without warning and leave in the same way. When the pains came, they would knock me to my knees. Within a few weeks I was advised that I needed a hysterectomy.

Masculine-dominated ideas were still prevalent in my life – so if my male doctor told me that this was what I needed and he assured me that I would suffer no "real" consequences, then I figured I should do it. I did ask him if I could keep my ovaries, but he just smiled and told me not to worry – that what he was advising was the best route. The doctor said that removing the uterus and the ovaries would not be a problem, that I really didn't need them now that my child-bearing days were over.

But guess what – I did need them. Taking the uterus and ovaries from my body threw my system into total shock. My whole physical and psychic system responded with a *"How could you!"* My thyroid and immune system rebelled. I felt broken. For many years I had taught others about unity, wholeness, empowerment, and oneness – and here I was feeling fragmented, torn asunder, and ripped apart internally. The ordeal went on for months, but all the while the Divine Mother was working with me, uncovering more of who She was and who I truly was as a part of Her.

The whole thing was a paradox. The gift in the experience was that in the midst of intense pain, I found a deeper sense of the warm, compassionate, safe, and all-embracing love of the Feminine nature of the Divine. I was carried into a crucible of transformation that contained what felt like a burning, scorching fire, and paradoxically it felt as if the Mother were gently taking me by the hand and guiding me where I needed to go. The Feminine nature of the Divine was forcibly pushing me – to learn to move with the rhythmic sway of the universal energies. She was asking me to move forward in my growth, and at the same time She was asking me to stand perfectly still.

Standing still in the midst of chaos and trust – this was a new concept for me. After all, I had learned well in life how to be the good, forward-marching, always-in-control, never-let-them-see-you-sweat, patriarchal daughter. But suddenly I had been brought to me knees. Nothing of the life I knew before seemed to fit. I was becoming "little" in order to become humble, and in the midst of this, I was learning the dance of the Feminine nature of the Divine. I was learning a new way of being.

My healing was about honoring who I was and the "sacred wounds" of life that I had experienced. I began to bless my body and to honor that I was female and that feminine energies and the ways of being a woman had worth and value – beyond that of child bearing.

Living Archetypal Energy

The more I delved into the ways of and the consciousness of the feminine nature of the Divine (the Feminine nature of the Divine, is a living archetypal energy – an archetypal energy is a pattern of thought that is held in the collective unconscious mind, and its energy affects us all), the more

She opened Her heart to me and taught me of Her ways. These archetypal energies, came to me in the form of ancient goddesses and shared their gifts and secrets with me.

Kali taught (no, *forced*) me to face my "human virtues" and my human limitations and transform all aspects of my being.

Hecate showed me the crossroads of life and guided me as to where and when to turn. She also took me by the hand and led me into and through the labyrinth of the underworld – the subconscious mind and my shadow selves – teaching me in the process ever-deeper lessons about who I am as a divine being.

Isis shared Her secrets of transformation and taught me how to fly, right where I was. She carried me forward with new wings.

The Black Madonna opened new vistas of awareness that allowed me to explore the deepest, darkest shadows of my being and as a result helped me reclaim my true voice.

Shakti revealed to me the play of the universe, its paradoxes and its wholeness.

Each one shared her gifts and her love, and through their generosity I found wholeness. I danced the dance of light and dark, of death and rebirth, of the shadow and the transformed, of grace and resistance, of sitting still and moving frantically.

Being fully in their presence, in awe and waiting for their lessons and directions, I held in my heart the words "I am in no hurry – I will sit and wait in peace for your guidance."

Oneness, wholeness, unity, completeness – life is about growth, and growth comes through the challenges and opportunities we experience in life. How we respond to them is the key determining our inner growth and ultimate sanity. Inherent in the desire for growth is the core idea of change. Change is inevitable – for we are to learn that the shadows are nothing more than sheer illusion. The desire to know our oneness calls forth the experiences of change.

We are in a constant state of remembering and of forgetting, of reuniting and of tearing apart. Life is change, and change is unpredictable, so I continue to breathe. What does the Feminine nature of the Divine want from me and from you? To do exactly this – to breathe, one breath after another, in the midst of all the trials and tribulations of life – keep breathing.

Toni G. Boehm

And somehow in the midst of that space of breathing, we are changed, transformed and renewed, for we learn to consciously embrace life's present moment fully – thus facilitating the creation of our journey to wholeness. Reclaiming the Feminine nature of the Divine isn't only for women. It is for all of us, male and female alike – for we are the "both/and" – we are the two in one.

The "Burning Experience" of the Feminine Nature of the Divine

The "burning experience" of the Feminine nature of the Divine is not just a one-time thing. It occurs over and over again until – I guess there is no until – for even Jesus was being "burned in the fires of transformation" up until the end of His life as we know it.

With this thought in mind, I share with you another experience of mine over a six-month period in 1999. The experience took shape like this:

If people are fortunate, once or twice in their lifetimes, destiny will permit them to cross paths with an *"idea or an individual"* that will transform their lives at depth and change their lives forever. I have been blessed with having experienced both – a life changing idea and an individual who helped change the course of my life forever.

I met the Divine Mother and She touched my heart and mind, shifting me at the core level of my being in the way I think, feel, and live. And I met and befriended one of the greatest teachers of our time on the role of the Divine Mother and Her influence on the evolution of consciousness: the prolific author Andrew Harvey.

Allow me to share how as I was being birthed by the Divine Mother into a new state of consciousness and way of being in life, Andrew Harvey appeared and helped me through this genesis process. This genesis was an agonizing yet bliss-filled and transformative experience of the heart, which birthed in me into a deeper, richer, and more profound understanding of the Feminine's nature of the Divine role in conscious evolution. It happened like this:

In January 1999, my friend Priscilla Richards brought a tape to me and told me that it contained a message that I must listen to. Priscilla is the director of a metaphysical library, so when she infers that there is some article, book, or tape that is "alive" with spiritual energy, my ears perk up. I honor her spiritual countenance and the wisdom that flows from her.

What she brought to me – delivered right to my doorstep – was a tape by Andrew Harvey, from his *Radiant Heart* album. I was familiar with Andrew's work, for through the years I had read many of his books.

When I finally had the time to sit down and listen to the tape, I was unprepared for what was about to happen. He was speaking of the Sacred Feminine and Her return into the conscious mind of humankind. In a flash, something deep within me resonated to these words. It was as if the Divine Feminine Herself were speaking to me from the depths of the cellular level of my being. I knew I had to speak with Andrew.

It did not take long for that thought to become a reality, for when something is meant to be, doors open effortlessly. Within a few hours, Andrew and I were on the phone having a discussion about the Divine Feminine. I shared the longings of my heart, my desire to know more of the Divine Mother and of sacred ways. Our conversation was animated and blazed with a holy energy. For the more than an hour we shared like this, it felt as if I my spirit were being given a drink of living water.

This living water was quenching a thirst that had for so long kept me feeling parched and dried at the very core of my being. A deep connection was made between Andrew and me in that moment. And little did I know what the Divine Mother had in store for me as an answer to my prayer to know more of who She was as a living presence.

In March, a nagging feeling began to make itself known to me. It was a feeling that "my container didn't fit any longer." I didn't know what that meant, but I was starting to be mighty uncomfortable. Nothing seemed to "work" for me. Old ways of doing things and old ways of being were all of a sudden feeling very foreign to me. My prayers started to became very dry and unfulfilling. My spirit and spiritual life, which had been my source of grounding for so long, were no longer able to provide me with the ususal "warm fuzzies."

Day by day, the feelings of uncomfortableness began to grow and grow, until after about two months, I knew that I was in a total meltdown. I didn't understand it, yet I felt as if I could stand back and observe the process. Also, I knew that there was nothing I could do about it. I was melting down; my old ways of living were not working for me any longer. I didn't know what to do or which way to turn. All the familiar things that had come so easily to me were so difficult that I could barely move. My boundless energy bounded off in another direction. I was so afraid that

Toni G. Boehm

someone might see what was happening to me and perceive that I was weak.

Yes, I was in meltdown; it was a disintegration of "the little me" on a level deeper than I had ever experienced before. I had proclaimed that I was on a journey with the Divine Mother to find out who I was as the feminine nature of the Divine and that I was being taken on a ride beyond anything I had ever imagined.

I tried desperately to hold it all together, then finally I reached a point were I had to stop and just surrender. I surrendered all of me, for that is what She wanted. I had to give up my pride, the pride of being the brave, good, perfect daughter for the "patriarchal" system, and I had to admit that I was helpless. It was devastating to my ego, yet I knew I had no choice. The Divine Mother wanted all of me, and She was relentless. I went to the "organizational powers that be" and I asked for a leave of absence from work. I needed time off to regroup. I could no longer keep up the facade. I was done pretending, She wanted me and I was ready to surrender – but I was scared to death.

I had never felt this out-of-control. I was always the one who could be counted on. I was "the strong one," "bossy," "assertive," "aggressive," "ambitious," "determined," "feisty," "forward," "intimidating," "a powerful woman,"— and these were just a few of the kinder words that had been used to describe me in my work environments.

During this time of total dissolution, disintegration, dissolving, merging, and re-emergence, Andrew called me every day. He labeled himself my "spiritual nanny." He would tell me: "Listen to your nanny now. He knows where you are and what you can do." He shared words of comfort and truth with me.

"My darling," he would whisper like a mother speaking to her beloved child, "you are being scorched in the Mother's fire in order that you might shine. Trust Her and Her work. You are being burned that your heart might heal the wounds that have been inflicted upon you by the consciousness of the world. You are suffering that you might be set free. For only a moment, you are being bound in what feels like hell so that you might dance in heaven."

Andrew gave me courage to walk through this time. He told me I was the birther and that I was also the one being birthed. I remembered from my nursing days that there is a point in the labor process known as the transition phase. If there is ever a time you need a coach during the birthing experience, the transition phase is it. During this time the birthing coach stays right with you to remind you when and how to breathe. The coach helps you stay focused and not give up – as if you could! Andrew was that coach for me during my time of transition. There were times during that "dark night and burning experience" when I felt that Andrew was not only telling me when to breathe but also providing me with the breath of the Mother's love.

Andrew sums up the bliss, suffering, blessing, and sacrifice of this birthing time with the Divine Mother in his book *The Teachings of Rumi*. Rumi states, *" the sweetness of the place of peace is proportionate to the pain of the journey."*

May all who ever grow through a sacred experience with the Divine Mother be blessed to have a coach like Andrew Harvey.

What I realize now is that these two experiences that I have just described were interrelated in regards to my soul growth and yet totally different, in the way of what was occurring within the context of the lesson. The first experience was a physical and a mental stripping, the second was an emotional burning and both used the body-in-breakdown as the vehicle for the lesson.

The first brought me face to face with the realization that spiritual transcendence alone is not the path to regeneration or the fullness of consciousness. I had been on the spiritual path for many years and meditated daily for hours. I realize now that my desire in meditation was to rise above the human level. I was perhaps, what one might call, spiritually arrogant. I had bought the transcendent, absolute realm of spirituality, hook line and sinker, and I was ready to forgo earth and to transcend. My physical challenge brought me back into the awareness of my body and its importance as vehicle in the process of spiritual growth and regeneration.

Fillmore in the *Revealing Word*, defines *regeneration* as *"a change in which abundant spiritual life, even eternal life, is incorporated into the body ... The transformation that takes place through bringing all the forces of mind and body to the support of the Christ ideal."*

Remember that after the transfiguration Jesus did not ascend. He came down from the mountain and eventually had to face the Crucifixion. There comes a time on the spiritual path when the disciple realizes that the transfiguring, transcendent, masculine face of God is only one of the points on the journey.

My second experience was an emotional and mental stripping of my

Toni G. Boehm

personality and my many attachments. In other words, I had to move from a Saul to a Paul consciousness. Paul means little and that is what we must do – become little, become humble. When you are stripped of everything that has defined who you are and you are unable to move or think, it is a very humbling experiencing. It is not about things being taken from you in the outer; it is about an inner stripping process that has nothing to do with the outer.

The Inner Stripping

Charles Fillmore speaks of this personality-stripping experience in his 1930s writings "The Hidden Man of the Bible." It appeared as an article entitled, *"The Hidden Man of the Bible: Woman,"* in *Weekly Unity*, June 23, 1912.

"Mary [Mary Magdalene is], the devotional side of the soul ... When the soul is lifted up in prayer and thanksgiving, there follows an out-flow of love which fills the "whole house," or body, with its odor. The anointing of the feet [when Mary Magdalene anoints Jesus' feet at the banquet] *represents the willingness of love [the devotional side of the soul] to serve [to provide whatever type of life experience is necessary for soul growth]...*

"Love is the 'greatest thing in the world,' according to Henry Drummond, who analyzed it in a masterly manner. Jesus acknowledged the power of love when he said, 'Suffer [would you have] *her* [Mary Magdalene] *to keep it* [the ointment of the outpouring of love] *against the day of my burying."* [Pour freely of love now! Be willing to consciously begin the redemptive and regenerative process now!]

"When personality is hurt to the death [when one experiences a devastating life experience or a spiritual "dark night of the soul"] *and surrenders all* [when personality – the adverse ego – renders itself vulnerable and says, 'not my will but Thy will be done,' and thus releases, lets go, and gives itself over to the greater power that lives within], *love pours her balm over every wound and the substance of her sympathy* [compassion] *infuses hope and faith to the discouraged soul."*

Mary Magdalene's Prayer
The Society of Saint Mary Magdalene
(adapted)

Mary Magdalene, you looked upon the face of Christ

And gazed upon the reflection of God.

You heard the voice of the Holy Spirit and

Forgiveness overflowed as love leaped in your soul ...

Mary, pour the oil of forgiveness onto me

And then pour the oil of love into my heart.

Pour Christ's cup of blessing into me – and into all ...

Pour Christ's cup of passion and compassion into me – and into all ...

Pour the contents of your alabaster jar upon the earth

With each tear crying, "Thy Kingdom come!"

Toni G. Boehm

All of Me, You Say?

Twisted and curled, I lie upon the couch, like a fetal ball awaiting birth. Sadness fills every cell of my being, and tears brim at the edges of my eyes. My tears are like clouds, full and ready to release their liquid drops upon a dry earth. Tears once released, seem to bring relief to my parched soul, if only for a moment.

Yet somehow in the sadness, there is a knowing that from this time of [sacred] darkness, there is a new way of living life that desires to be born through me. I am aware that no matter how much I want to, I cannot force this delivery. Like one who is nine months pregnant, I can only wait for the appointed time of delivery. Days turn into weeks and the heaviness of "pregnancy" pervades my every thought and action.

"Now, God?" I groan. "What is it that you want from me?" I pause, waiting for an answer. I hear nothing! I cry out again, "What do you want from me?" "Has God left me?" I ponder in the sadness of my heart.

"All of you," I hear.

"What did you say?" I query.

Again an inner voice speaks to me, "I said that I want all of you!"

"But I have given you all of me. How much more do you want?"

(I whine these words like a little child demanding to have its own way.)

The voice stops. I hear it no more! Into the silence I retreat, for this seems to be the only place of refuge for me in this time of personal crisis. There are no computers, televisions, or telephones; there is no one to talk to except my own inner thoughts and the Holy Spirit – the Holy Mother. Drawn by a force unlike anything I have experienced in my day-to-day existence to date, I am compelled to sit and listen. I listen to the trees, to the wind, to the birds, to the sky, to the flowers, to all forms of nature. I ponder how it is that I can take time to meditate daily but have never taken time to listen to the trees. I think about my daily routine and I realize that often, once my day gets started, I barely take time to a take a break.

Hours go by. I am mesmerized by this state of silence. Suddenly, Sister Wind whispers to me through the rustle of the swaying branches and sings Her words to me through the trees: "I have a message for you. Listen deeper ... listen deeper ... listen deeper." Sister Wind's melody draws me into the recesses of me soul. Sister Wind's words are reminiscent of a familiar passage I first heard long ago: "I stand in the presence of God and I have been sent to speak to you, to give you the Good News." Now I know that Sister Wind has been sent by God to stand before me and speak to me of the Good News.

Sister Wind enrolls the winged ones in the message's deliverance. A cacophony of sound fills my ears and heart, a symphony prepared for me and only for me. A new sense of joy and aliveness wells up within me as I ponder.

"How is it that in the midst of the appearance of such travails in my life, with the feeling that the outer world is pressing in on me from all sides ... how is it that I can find shelter from myself within myself?"

I cry as the answer is revealed to me. "Nearer than hands and feet I am, ready with a sacred embrace when you say 'Yes' and respond with the willingness to surrender your all to Me."

In the quiet sanctuary of nature, I find a part of myself again. "Go ye apart awhile and drink of the living water – this is good for the soul," my Spirit says. Sister Wind rustles the branches of the trees, as if she is nodding her head in approval. The songbirds and geese chime in to signal their agreement. I marvel at Mother nature and Her many miracles.

The day is overcast; the clouds are ripe and ready to deliver their goods. I laugh as I realize that the metaphor of the sun hiding its face is a reflection of my own behavior, for I have been hiding mine, lo, these many months.

Wrapped in a blanket to protect me from the cool air, I feel a chill ripple through my body, a body that for several months has been wracked with the emotional pain, that often accompanies the process of transformation and the feeling of being isolated from God. Suddenly I realize that a part of me has died but it was only so that another part of me could find a new life. Sadness, grief, isolation, and despair were my teachers, and I acknowledge them for the teachers that they have been over these last few weeks and months. It is clear that I no longer desire to live life as I have before, so "dying" is good.

The journey into the (sacred) darkness has been a tough, but good one. It has taken me to my inner depths, where I have made friends with fears – fears that expressed themselves as a need to be in control, to appear perfect, and in a multitude of other ways of being that I had hidden away beneath a veneer of trying to appear cool, calm, collected, and in control.

As afraid as I was of these fears, the gift I received when I faced them was that they taught me I desire to live and see life differently. Through facing

Toni G. Boehm

my "adversaries," I made a new friend and her name is Compassion. And sweet Compassion has given me the greatest gift of all – Compassion has given me the gift of knowing and loving my own true Self!

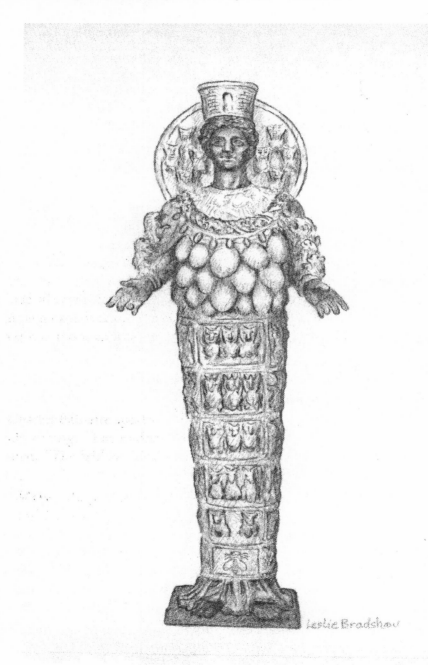

Leslie Bradshaw

~ Chapter Nine ~

Mystery and Mysticism: The Essence of the
Feminine Nature of the Divine

" ... prayer is more than asking God for help in the physical world;
it is in its highest sense the opening up in our soul of an innate
spiritual umbilical cord that connects us with the Holy Mother,
from which we can receive a perpetual flow of life.
This [connection] is the beginning of eternal life
for both soul and body, the essential teaching of Jesus,
which he demonstrated in overcoming death."

- Myrtle Fillmore
Teach Us to Pray

We discussed in the earlier chapters the return of the Feminine nature of the Divine to conscious mind. Her return is being seen in many ways, one of the most profound of which is a message that has been given to all the people of the Catholic Church by Pope John Paul II. The Pope on October 8, 2000, consecrated this new millennium to Our Lady, the Blessed Mother. His personal motto is "totus tuus," which means that he belongs totally to the Mother and that he is asking everyone else to do the same.

The Pope says this about the Mother: *"I entrust this responsibility of the whole Church to the maternal intercession of Mary [the Divine Feminine] ... She ... will be for Christians on the way to the Great Jubilee of the Third Millennium the Star that safely guides their steps."*

Friends, this is a reason for celebration! Rejoice and be glad for we know that the Divine Mother is an energy force, not a living being, and She/It is bringing Herself into awareness through the activity of the conscious mind. Remembering - having an awareness of an issue, problem, condition, and so on - is the first step in healing. First, we have to be aware that there is an issue before the issue can be resolved. Therefore, having this proclaimed as the millennium of the Holy Mother is no accident.

It is the Divine Feminine's way of coming forward out of the darkness of the hidden recesses of the unconscious mind. Soon She will be remembered

Toni G. Boehm

for who She truly is, co-creator with the Divine Masculine. She is coming forth arrayed in Her own "special clothing." This clothing is a new way of seeing and living life, from the perspective of a unified or integrated spirituality, a joining of the Divine Masculine and the Divine Feminine in consciousness. Although this thought will be dressed in the facade of the pomp, circumstance, and pageantry of a declaration of a millennium dedicated to a Mother who lived 2000 years ago, Her true message will seep through into conscious awareness.

Behind that facade of this outer picture of pageantry is the energy of the Divine Mother, the archetypal Divine Feminine waiting to reclaim Her place in the mind of humankind. The Divine, Cosmic Feminine of the book of Revelation is desiring to come forth in Her splendor and glory; as the shining example of the Motherhood of God. The time is coming when the authority of the Divine Feminine will be restored and She will take Her place within the conscious awareness of humankind. I believe that the time is now and that Her deepest desire is for us to awaken to the Glory which lives within us and be willing to receive the gifts She has to offer.

"I am a Chalice for the re-birth of the Feminine Nature of the Divine. I am a Chalice of Sacred Fire."

— Priscilla Richards (adapted)

"The Authority of the Divine Feminine Restored"

Charles Fillmore shares this belief and eloquently discusses the restoration of Her authority in a Sunday lesson that he gave on January 16, 1916. This lesson is entitled, *The Authority Of The Divine Feminine Restored.*

"The first step ... If you would enter into the secret of the mind of Spirit, you must repent; and repentance is simply a change of viewpoint. Instead of looking at things through the little hole which your ancestors looked through, or that you have set up in your own narrow [mind] ... Repent from those sins of limitation [instead of being stuck in your **narrow views of religion, life or spirituality as you have known them, be willing to repent, to open your mind to the possibility of other ways of seeing things**].

"We are all limited by our own thoughts, and we never will get the great freedom of God ... Mind until we are willing to let go and humble ourselves ... We must let go of this idea that the intellectual man, the

man of the world, the outer successes of man, have any element of success in them. They are not under the Law.

"The only Law is Divine Law, and before [we] can know that Law there must be a humble state of mind; In other words, you must repent of that sin state of intellectual egotism; that knowing-it-all.

"There is in the feminine mind an intuitive something that the intellectual man does not possess ... We know that man [humankind] is [both] masculine and feminine; when man, the one who is expressing the masculine, comes to an understanding of the Spirit, he becomes more intuitive; his love-nature is developed.

"And so the woman, when she comes into spiritual understanding and the Law begins its adjustment in her, she becomes more forceful and directive ... We are in our present civilization coming to a place where the whole human family, and especially the masculine part of the human family, must recognize the Divine Feminine.

"There must be a lifting up of that spiritual quality in the dominant race thought ... There must be a lifting up into the realm of intuition, of love, of tenderness, those qualities which belong supremely to the woman. We can see that this movement is becoming universal ...

"What is the true relation existing between the masculine and the feminine in the doctrine of Jesus Christ; in pure Christianity; What might be called esoteric Christianity - the spiritual side of the Christian Religion?

"Jesus said when the question was put to him - 'Who shall be the husband of this wife in the Resurrection?' (She had seven husbands.) He answered: 'In the Kingdom of God there is neither marrying nor giving in marriage. You do not understand the Scripture.' This by metaphysicians has been construed to mean that in the new relation, the new kingdom of restitution which we discern is now coming into expression, there will be no marriage.

"But did Jesus mean that? You will remember that in another place in the Scripture he said: 'Know ye not that he created you in his image and likeness, male and female, and for this cause shall a man leave his father and his mother and cleave unto his wife, and they twain shall let no man put asunder.'

"This is a stronger passage than the other, and it means that there is a divine marriage. In the former statement he was referring to the outer.

Toni G. Boehm

He was referring to these marriages by Magistrates and Justices of the Peace performed for men and women.

"But there is a marriage of Spirit; there is a union of men and women. That is, the [inner] *masculine and* [the inner] *feminine - those qualities which exist in being -* [in humankind, where every man is female and male and every woman is female and male] *... We cannot escape this conclusion* [that there is both an inner and outer union of masculine and feminine complements].

"We [also then] *cannot escape the conclusion that Jesus Christ himself had a wife. But you say there is not a record of it. There is a record of his having loved Martha and Mary ... He loved Mary. She was his Divine Feminine in personal manifestation. She represents the Divine Feminine which [required] purification. (The seven devils were cast out of her.)*

"Mary anointed his feet with oil. She wept over him. She loved him. Mary was the first at the sepulcher; she was there before daylight looking for her Lord's body. And she said to what she supposed was the gardener: 'They have taken him away.' He spoke to her and said: 'Mary, why weepest thou?'

"Now, if there has not been something a little closer than the love of friends between these two, why should she have taken such a vital, loving interest in Jesus? Why should she have claimed his body? What right had she? He had relatives; it was their right to take charge of that body. So, we discern that Mary was the wife of Jesus Christ.

"That may be a startling proposition. But when you see the union of soul with soul - when you see that inner marriage which exists between two people that are in harmony you realize the great Truth that there never was a man nor a woman but what there was somewhere the complement; there was somewhere that other soul that when these two were joined in spirit everything moves in Divine Order ...

"The Divine Feminine must be brought into expression ... There must be an equalization, an adjustment, a righteousness between men and women in all affairs ... Nothing is too small in business to be excluded from the consultation of that intuitive knowledge which a woman has ... it is the Divine Feminine in the woman that brings this power into finances.

"Why should there be such a relation between a financial success and

the Divine Feminine, or the intuitive love of the woman? Because love is the substance. Love is really the substance back of all money. And that is why the man in order to be successful ... must have the co-operation of the Divine Feminine ... We are told that after Napoleon had divorced Josephine, he had no further success. He had separated himself from that great, enfolding substance of love, and no man can demonstrate what we call immortality of soul and body unless he has the co-operation of the Divine Feminine.

"Not only must you awaken that in your soul, but you must establish such a quality of manhood [humbleness] that you can have the co-operation of ... woman ... through the union of the man and woman there shall come a new quality; there will be a quickening of power, mental, spiritual, and physical. The great uplifting stream in man's conscious-ness, in his body, is LOVE - Divine Love; and that stream must be lifted; it must not be dissipated in sensation. There must be a new standard fixed, and that standard is Spirit ...

"Now, I would say to my brother man -`let us get down off our high horse, let us be humble and willing to accept the intuitive word of the Divine Feminine, in every affair of our lives; let us take their intuition, their perception of things into whatever we do, and I assure you we will achieve success; a restitution of our mind ... Deep down in human consciousness is the wonderful Law, and it is only revealed when we let go and give ourselves up, and hold ourselves as one with Spirit - the Spirit of God manifests in Masculine and Feminine.

Toni G. Boehm

Exercise:
Traversing the Labyrinth

"Truth is on the march and nothing can stop it."
- Emile Zola

All paths lead to the center.
- T.G.B.

Purpose: Centering, clearing, empowerment, inspiration

Setting: Individual inner-work

Materials: Copies of finger labyrinth, (see pg.___) and a journal and pen

Note: Excerpts from this labyrinth section were a collaborative effort between, author, Rosemary Ellen Guiley and myself.

The labyrinth is recognized as an ancient symbol, for the Feminine nature of the Divine, it represents the cycles of life, death, and rebirth. It is a walking meditation revered since ancient times as an archetypal mandala for a journey of consciousness, a search for knowledge and truth, a mental focusing tool, "a playground for allowing intuition to take flight," and for its transformative nature and healing powers. Although its origins are mysterious and unknown, it has been traced back, in the various forms that it has taken over the past several thousand years, to areas such as Greece (Crete and Knossos), Europe (France), Egypt, Indonesia, Peru, Iceland, and other cultures throughout the world.

The motif of the labyrinth has appeared in mythology, architecture, art, dance, rites, and rituals. The triple spiral, a precursor to the pattern found on the labyrinth, was used in both eastern and western Europe as a design on pottery and at sacred burial places as early as 14,000 B.C.E. The oldest surviving labyrinth, dating to c. 2500 B.C.E., appears on a rock carving at Luzzanas on the island of Sardinia, Italy. Fragments of labyrinth designs can be traced back to 6500 B.C.E. The Egyptians, Greeks, Celts, and Indians made great use of them. Labyrinths were built by these various cultures, for they were believed to be portals to the spirit world, which when contacted brought a sense of centeredness and calmness.

A labyrinth, although it has been mislabeled at times as a maze, is not a maze! A maze has many possible paths that one can choose from within its complicated design. If people make an incorrect decision, they will move onto a path that leads to nowhere, a dead end. This can leave the traveler feeling a sense of bewilderment, internally chaotic and distracted.

The pattern of a labyrinth is said to be based on the principles of sacred geometry. Linda Eileen Sewright in her article, *"Rites of Passage: The Labyrinth and the Consciousness of the Land,"* speaks of this concept: ***"Sacred geometry ... is the pattern of numbers that is inherent in nature and in the patterns of the stars. It is the dance of atoms by which spirit infuses matter and by which the planets orbit the sun. To construct a labyrinth using these principles [of sacred geometry] is to invoke our inherent wholeness and evolutionary pattern. It is the human in concert with the mysteries and sacred patterns of the universe."***

After having the privilege and pleasure of personally walking one of the most famous labyrinths on earth - the one at Chartres Cathedral in Chartres, France - and now owning my own, I have my own insights and thoughts about this sacred motif and the internal process that occurs within as one circumnavigates its winding path.

As I was walking the labyrinth at Chartres, the process, in and of itself, allowed me to tap into a deeper reservoir of living water contained within the well of my heart. I was being saturated with energy - a pulsating, vibrating, rhythmic and throbbing palpable force was moving within my cellular structure. And on some level, I felt connected to the essence of the universe, my ancient ancestors, and my own interior wisdom.

Traversing those sacred circuits, I was magically being moved out of a consciousness of "doing" something and being eased into a deeper experience of "being." The sacred geometry inherent within the design of the labyrinth wound me back and forth, from left to right, then right to left, rebalancing my interior brain and cellular system with each step. It felt as if I were being offered the opportunity to synchronize my body, my masculine and feminine aspects, allowing them to intermingle, intertwine, reacquaint, and recoordinate. All of this was happening simultaneously. With each footstep there was a refocusing and a reflecting on the patterns of my life.

The labyrinth seemed to act as a focusing lens that brought my collective unconscious into focus on a personal level, while at the same time it seemed I was being aligned with the greater forces at work in the universe. It felt as if an inner activation of all of my faculties was taking place. When I reached the entrance to the center of this sacred circle, I consciously made my way

Toni G. Boehm

to the first of the six petals that surrounded the center point. Moving from petal to petal in a state of conscious awareness, I felt as if I were stripping away layers of cellular muck and mire that had accumulated over lifetimes. Once having traversed all six petals, I then stepped into the center of this sacred wheel. I entered in an upright position; then I was drawn to lie down with my arms stretched out and my heart resting over the very center, the heart of the labyrinth. I was in a state of total surrender, committing myself, my life, and whatever work I was to do in the world to the will and the work of the divine and especially to the Feminine nature of the Divine. The feeling I experienced in that moment was one of a reconstruction of my being at the deepest level of awareness. I have walked labyrinths on many occasions, and each time brings its own unique and personal experience of my humanness and of my divinity.

Laid out on the ground or a floor, the labyrinth is entered and walked in a circular fashion to its center and then exited by the same circular route. When we fully engage in the walk of the labyrinth, we experience a quieting of the mind, an opening of the heart, and an awakening of wholeness, oneness, and possibility. The labyrinth inspires change from within a deep level of the self. We experience a refreshing renewal that leads to peace of mind and clarity of thought.

The term labyrinth is believed to come from labrys, or the double axe, a symbol of the Greek god Zeus. The double axe was the symbol of power in the Minoan culture in ancient Crete, where labyrinths were especially prevalent.

In the Middle Ages, the labyrinth became a walking substitute for the sacred pilgrimage to the Holy Land. During the wars of the Crusades, from the eleventh to thirteenth centuries, journeys to the Holy Land were dangerous. The Roman Catholic Church designated seven cathedral labyrinths in Europe as acceptable replacements that would offer the same spiritual renewal as an actual pilgrimage. Walking the labyrinth gave pilgrims the experience of communion with the ultimate reality: the knowledge of Self, and the knowledge that God and Self are one. The most famous labyrinth still remaining is on the floor of the Cathedral at Chartres, France.

When the Renaissance ushered in the Age of Science, labyrinths began to decline in importance. They faded from spiritual practice. In recent years, the labyrinth has been revived and greeted with tremendous enthusiasm, as people once again have connected with the power of the path. In the United States, the Reverend Dr. Lauren Artress, cannon of special ministries at

Grace Cathedral Church in San Francisco and author of Walking the Sacred Path, created a labyrinth at her church that has drawn more than one million visitors from all over the world. Artress describes the labyrinth's path as a metaphor for our own spiritual journeys. All you have to do is follow the path, and it will take you inward.

The labyrinth has no dead ends or wrong turns, but has one path that leads to the center. Thus it represents the mystery of the soul's journey to the mystic center. The path does not go directly to the center, but takes a meandering, circular route that enables the traveler to go through distinct shifts in consciousness along the way. From the center, the same path leads out. This represents the return to the world, in which the gifts of illumination are brought back to be manifested in life.

The labyrinth symbolizes the journey of regeneration and enlightenment found in many religious traditions. In Christianity, this journey is called "union with God." In Buddhism, it is "the path to enlightenment," and in Hinduism "the path to freedom." In mythology, it is a symbol of humankind's dual nature, for one walks it through his or her active masculine aspect while being guided by his or her more passive, intuitive feminine nature.

A labyrinth laid out on company grounds can be visited at any time by employees seeking inspiration or a recharging of their batteries. Labyrinths are being placed in the workplace, for they are recognized as powerful tools for individual centering and clearing, helping to release stress, quiet the mind, and reveal the still center within. When the mind is quieted and cleared, one is better able to see situations objectively and is open to flashes of intuition that help to solve problems and create new ideas.

At the California Pacific Medical Center, Dr. Martin Brotman initially was dubious that walking a labyrinth could produce such results. "I overcame my skepticism and installed the labyrinth in the hospital setting," he said. "A lot of our patients and families and staff say it helps them deal with stress."

For example, cardiac patients use it to recover from their surgery. Said one patient, "As I got into it, all of a sudden my mind became very peaceful." Breast cancer patients have used it as a way to deal with pain and uncertainty. A woman said that as she walked the path, "I was thinking, wondering if I were still going to be here in ten years - now I'm sure of that."

Toni G. Boehm

Just as powerful, and more convenient, as "her" walking counterpart is the portable finger labyrinth, a simplified version of the one at Chartres. The route is traced with a finger, a pencil or perhaps a colored pen. The key to the labyrinth is the intent of the person; results do not depend on whether the labyrinth is "finger" walked or traced. The finger labyrinth is small and portable, therefore, it can be kept close at hand for use in those moments when life becomes overwhelming and a sense of clarity and calmness is desired.

There are three stages to walking the labyrinth:

Stage 1: Entering the labyrinth. As you walk to the center, focus on the releasing, emptying, and quieting of negative thoughts. Relinquish the things you have sought to control and the worries that control you, and surrender yourself to the journey. If annoying thoughts keep intruding, gently see them being swept away - do not try to resist them or dismiss them. Travel the path slowly. Have no expectations - only an open mind and an open heart ready to receive the gifts of the labyrinth. Openness is a powerful tool for generating energy.

In mystical terms, this stage is called "purgation," which is the release of all things that block communication with our higher power. We cannot hear Truth when our minds are busy.

Stage 2: Entering the center. Many times reaching the center of the labyrinth comes as a surprise because of the winding, circular path. You don't know you're "there" until you're there - which reflects what oftentimes happens in life. The key to realizing life's potential is to be present to the moment. Most of us spend most of our time dwelling on the past or thinking about the future. While both activities do have their value at appropriate times, they limit our horizon and prevent us from unleashing new transformative energies. Only when we are present to the moment are we in contact with our full creative potential.

Once in the center of the labyrinth, be present to the moment. Do not be in a hurry to leave, for it is here that insight, the "aha!" of creativity, occurs. The gifts of the labyrinth reveal themselves in startling clarity. They may include insight into a problem or situation; new perspectives; creative ideas; and feelings of empowerment, integration, receptivity, authenticity, and self-confidence.

In mystical terms, this stage is called "illumination," which is the knowing of the sacred self within. We hear Truth.

Stage 3: Leaving the labyrinth. On the journey out, allow yourself to feel replenished, balanced, and empowered by your experience. Travel slowly here too, which will allow the new energies to take hold. Be absorbed in your self-revelation.

In mystical terms, this stage is called "union," which means communing with and being absorbed in God. We bring Truth into our being.

Following your exit from the labyrinth, spend some quiet time in meditation and reflection to integrate the experience. Record your experience and insights in your journal.

Walking the labyrinth is an alchemical process that continues to unfold. Like other forms of inner work, the labyrinth opens one up to new flows of energies. Pay attention to dreams and synchronicity, which can bring more information, wisdom. and ideas. Daily prayer and meditation also augment the labyrinth.

The experience of the labyrinth varies and ultimately depends upon the openness and willingness of the participant to fully engage in the process. The gifts of the labyrinth may be big or small, but each is profound in its own unique way.

I have conducted the labyrinth exercise many times and have witnessed numerous transformational experiences, such as breakthroughs in insights, attainment of inner peace, and inspirations for solutions to problems. People always enjoy this activity - they feel as though they are participating in something ancient and mystical.

Full-size labyrinths can be painted or drawn with chalk on floors or parking lots for temporary or permanent use. Portable labyrinths, printed on large cloths, can be rolled or folded for use almost anywhere. I own a portable labyrinth that is easy to transport, and what I have found is that when the labyrinth experience is designed into a retreat or workshop, the participants are often moved to tears as they traverse its sacred circuits for the first time, for it mystically opens an inner aspect of being.

Finger labyrinths can be copied onto a sheet of paper and are ready for use at any moment the need is felt, for there are times when the tension in our lives becomes a little formidable. This can happen because of interaction with other people, or it can happen when we feel stuck and wish we could get a shot of inspiration.

The following finger-labyrinth exercise can be done in the privacy of your home or at your desk. It can also be done in a group setting, such as at a retreat. Once you have "walked" the labyrinth, take note of how you are feeling and what sensations you are experiencing. In fact, you might journal your experience and then come back to your writings in a day or two and see what new insights, if any, you have received.

Chapter Ten

The Feminine Nature of the Divine Renews and Revitalizes Through the Regenerative Power of Divine Love

"Step out of the circle of time
and into the circle of love."
— Rumi

Jesus Christ is said to be a Way-Shower, but what was it that He truly came to show us, to teach us? That we are sinners? That we are unworthy? No! It was the idea of regeneration. – that through the right use of mind, in connection with the power of the Holy Spirit, we could release the sense of separation from God we feel and fully realign our energy with the Divine.

Charles Fillmore gives us an overview of the Feminine's role in regeneration as he shares his thoughts on the regenerative aspect of the Holy Spirit. These thoughts are from his January 27, 1929, Sunday lesson.

"Jesus Christ ... reached the limit of his masculine consciousness [note that this reference is not about gender, but is about qualities and attributes that Jesus recognized as imperative in His soul development] *and He said that he must go* [in a physical sense], *but in His place would come this Holy Spirit* [the Divine Feminine and Her unique qualities], *and that it was expedient that He go. If He didn't go in that personal way and dissolve Himself in Holy Spirit, we could not get that Spirit within us ... when He broadcast the atoms of ... His body, they became the property of the whole race ...*

"He was the light of the world, the heat of the world ... but He could not express Himself on that plane until He became the Holy Mother, until He was the Mother of us all ...

What does Fillmore mean here? What was his thinking behind these series of statements? Why is it that Jesus could not express Himself fully until He became the fullness of the Holy Mother? What does the Holy Mother or Holy Spirit have to do with this?

I believe that to find the answer to this question, we need to go to John 4:26, the story of Jesus and the Samaritan woman. Jesus is sharing who and what God is with the Samaritan woman. He tells her that God is Spirit and those who worship Him must worship Him in Spirit.

If Jesus is going to join in God's kingdom, then wouldn't it make sense that He, too, would have to be Spirit, be regenerated into a spiritual body? In order to take on the fullness of a spiritual body, He would have had to embody the fullness of the qualities of the Holy Spirit, the Holy Mother.

We are made in the image and likeness of God, but God is not corporeal. We will not or perhaps cannot live in the plane of energy that Fillmore is talking about with this physical body – at least not for any extended period of time. This physical body is provided to us as a workstation for our stay here on earth. It is the vehicle through which we are able to release layers of mental and emotional conditioning that have covered the mind and kept the glory of God from shining through. These layers of conditioning have also kept us from expressing the full spectrum of the light and heat of God.

It is only when the subconscious mind is clear that the glory can shine through. How do we clear the subconscious mind? Through the activity of the Holy Spirit working within us. This is not work that we can do on our own, because the subconscious holds not only our thoughts and beliefs but those of race consciousness. Jesus, through the activity of the Holy Spirit that descended upon Him at His baptism, began the first steps of this deep cleansing process and continued on with it throughout His life.

With each layer of muck that is removed, the light of Christ shines through. When we embody the fullness of the light, we will no longer need these physical workstations; we will work, live, and have our being in Spirit. In the meantime these corporeal vehicles are absolutely needed and important and necessary to the process of spiritual growth.

"We are joint heirs with Him ... Joint heirs to what? ... To the substance of the Father, to the power, to all of those dominant qualities that [have the ability if misused to] make us dictators.

When the masculine attributes of God are the only powers or qualities that are honored and respected by a society, those qualities have the potential to become unbalanced and thus ineffective spiritually. For instance, power – the masculine – -must be tempered or in union with love – the feminine – or else a person can become an aggressive dictator. Intelligence – the masculine – must be tempered with Love – the feminine – to have true wisdom.

"But have we realized that we are joint heirs to the love of the Father? And that is not really the father quality, as we conceive it. It is a

mother quality; so we must think about God as Mother as well as Father. We must think about and worship the Holy Mother and talk to the Holy Mother, and enter into that Holy Mother consciousness within us ... We have not that concept of the mother. We have to leave that old concept of a Job-like, stern God and get right down into the forgiving love of the Mother ...

"Saul represents will ... the personality is large, and the man who lives in his personal will always wants the things that go with personality ... He [King Saul] wanted to do the will and the work of God, but he did it like a king would do it, through arbitrary force, through the power of the will ... [on the other hand] Paul means little. He realized that in order to make himself receptive to the Divine Principle, this Spirit of God, he must become personally small.

"People say, 'How can I get the Holy Spirit?' ... You can't overcome the arrogance and the egotism and the greed and the selfishness, the jealousy and the anger, of the mortal man without the Holy Spirit. It can't be done. People say, 'I am perfectly willing to have this Holy Spirit work in me,' and they sit down and expect it to work without their doing anything ... if the mind is filled with greed and pride and selfishness and conceit, self-sufficiency and ambition, and all those things, is there any room in it for these other attributes? No. Then there must be an adjustment of consciousness.

[This is where the spiritual journey that Jesus revealed to us through his life comes in to play. The different phases and stages of Jesus' life provide us with a roadmap as to how to take on Christhood in consciousness. This journey is clearly spelled out for us in the four Gospels. From the Annunciation to the Ascension, we are given clues as to how to move into Christ consciousness. The road-map shares with us what things we must let go of, and it also shares a forecast of the pitfalls and the opportunities that we will encounter along the way. At each juncture on the journey, we are given the chance to make conscious choices as to whether we will say "yes" to the upward progressive movement of our soul.]

"So we Christian metaphysicians find that we can put on the Holy Spirit consciousness, but we must put off something before we do that. We must try to eliminate these lower attributes of the mind. We must get rid of our ambitions to shine personally, and you will find that as you begin to think about the Holy Spirit of God – that is what it means –

Toni G. Boehm

you lose part of your personal ambitions. That is good.

[Experiences that look like dark nights of the soul or crucifixions are "gifts" that come for the purpose of aiding us in the discovery of who we are, so count them good. Move through them with a sense of willingness, when they come, for truly these "testing" times come only after we have accumulated the resources in consciousness that will allow us to grow through them. Our responses to these experiences are our gauges of how much we have truly grown in consciousness.]

"Count everything as good that has entered into your life, when you once have entered into or made discovery of the Spirit of God, or the Divine Feminine; because you must become like Paul. You must become little. You must humble yourself, and when you do that you are exalted. [Paul] had to give it all up ... and he came without authority, without anything except this Spirit of God. There is no other way to get into eternal life but to cultivate the Holy Spirit. [Cultivate the attributes of the Holy Spirit. Consciously cultivate the qualitites of intuition, love, compassion, a forgiving heart, a nurturing spirit, humility, peace, equality, and meekness.]

"Jesus Christ, as a man, in form, was not holy. He released this divine energy. And we have locked up in these bodies, in every cell of our organism ... energy that we are told by our men of science, if [we] should release and let all the energy of one tear go at one time, it would blow over a six-story building ...

"And there is one of the greatest secrets of our evolution – the outpouring of this locked up energy and life in man, pouring out through the unifying with the Holy Spirit. Jesus taught that to the disciples on the day of Pentecost. What did they have? Tongues of fire; they had new ability, new fire, the result of Holy Spirit principle.

"This ability and this power, this upper room, is right here in every one of us. We don't have to go outside ... It is the upper story of your mind ... think about divine things ... and all at once you can feel a contact between that upper room [your head] and the love center [your heart] down in your body. Then you begin to realize those locked up elements ... in every little affair of your life, incorporate this Holy Spirit into that, whatever it may be ... know that the Way is the way of the Truth, it is the way of evolution, it is the way of the unfolding of the Spirit of God in men; and that is the work of the Holy Spirit."

At the beginning of this paragraph, Fillmore shares with us the idea of an upper room. At first, he is specifically speaking of the upper room where the disciples received the Holy Spirit, then he moves to the idea that the upper room is within us, in our upper mind. This upper room is a symbolic image that has been used by various spiritual traditions over many millennia. It refers to the place where we come into contact with the divine and connect with that sense of total oneness and unity.

This upper room has many names, some of which are the following: the seventh Chakra, seventh Chalice, the nuptial chamber, or the Upper Womb. Regardless of its name, it functions as a place where the Feminine nature of the Divine and the Masculine meet and unite to begin to do their mighty work in and through us.

Remember, the true work of the Holy Spirit is to release within us the love of the Holy Mother, the feminine aspect of God Energy. It is the greatest secret in our evolutionary process, the explosive power of Divine Love, and it is known by only a few.

Regeneration – The Ultimate Work of the Feminine Nature of the Divine

This activity of releasing the Holy Spirit within the body unites the Spirit, soul, and body in spiritual oneness. This is also known as regeneration, or taking on the spiritual body, and that is the ultimate effect of the work of the Divine Mother. When the energy of the Holy Spirit is released, the body is regenerated, renewed, restored, and revitalized into a whole new level of being. The key to regeneration, however, is the awakening of the Feminine nature of the Divine energies of love and compassion, which lie asleep within you.

Regeneration is a change that occurs within the body, in which abundant spiritual life is incorporated into every cell of your being. This change takes place by bringing all the forces of your mind and body into and under the support of your Higher Power. However, this transmutation can only take place through a consciousness that is willing to and holds the intention for surrender. This is not a surrendering to something or someone outside of yourself, but a giving over to the "Greater" within you of all the "lesser" that lives within your consciousness (for example, greed, jealousy, anger, addictions, etc.).

This clearing of consciousness happens through your active, intentional participation in spiritual disciplines such as the activities of affirmations and denials, forgiveness, meditation, and prayer. These purification exercises work first in the intellect, as a deeper instillation and awareness of the Truth behind the "moral" codes or laws of life. Continued discipline in these areas moves you into your emotional level of being, the plane of desire. It is on this level that you open the door for the Divine Feminine nature of being to make Her entrance into your heart and mind. This deep, conscious purification of consciousness prepares the way for the outpouring of the cleansing fire of the Holy Spirit, which initiates the process of regeneration.

The mighty fire of the Holy Spirit does Her work in the crucible of your heart, Her womb of change and creative workshop. It is the work of Her fire that ultimately creates the change of consciousness in you and in the world. Fire, Holy Spirit, divine love, the feminine aspect of God – regardless of what you call Her, Her only desire is to release the fullness of the regenerative power that lives within you.

Charles Fillmore shares in *The Revealing Word* his beliefs on love and compassion. : Love is *"the Pure essence of Being that binds together the whole human family ... Love is the power that joins and binds in divine harmony the universe and everything in it; the great harmonizing principle known to man ... Whoever calls upon God as Holy Spirit for healing is calling on divine love. Divine love will bring your own to you ... and make your life and affairs healthy, happy, harmonious and free, 'Love therefore is the fulfillment of the law' (Rom. 13:10)."*

Compassion is *"a characteristic of love and mercy prompted by an understanding heart. A compassionate heart sees the error, but does not condemn ... [See John 8:11: 'Neither do I condemn you ... go and sin no more.'] In the heart of God exists an eternal tenderness and mercy for His children."*

As the Feminine nature of the Divine and Her qualities of equality, harmony, interconnectedness, compassion for one another, and so on, were repressed, the intellectual aspect of the Masculine nature of the Divine was elevated. The results of this repression ultimately produced in the psyche of humankind a lack of development of the love nature. The mind was given dominance at the expense of the heart. Perhaps this is why the Genesis story is called "The Fall, " because we fell out of balance in both our spiritual and physical states of being.

Although the Feminine nature of the Divine has been and continues to be held in a state of repression in the consciousness of humankind, Her energy does not go anywhere. She continues to try to make Herself known. However, since humankind is not willing to allow Her to reveal Her energy in its positive nature, the energy gets subverted into negative features, known as projection and shadow expression.

This shadow side of love characterizes and reveals itself in the consciousness of humankind as selfishness; a "me first" attitude; an unbalanced and convoluted emotional nature; chaos and turbulence expressing as warlike activities between nations and conflict that leads to killing in the name of righteousness and religious freedom; an attitude that "my way" is the right way; physical abuse of spouses and children because there is a feeling of "ownership"; a feeling of the right to hurt one of a "lesser" stature; and children joining gangs just to feel a sense of belonging, a sense of love. These are but just a few scenarios that come out of a dearth of the nurturing aspect of Divine Love in consciousness.

Everything that appears in this world is a result of a greater law at work. That law is the law of Divine Love, God expressing in Its unchanging spiritual nature as the Divine Feminine. In this form, Divine Love is, as Fillmore says, *"the spiritual glue that binds together the universe."* The consciousness of humankind is bankrupt and devoid of the one binding principle that is forever at its disposal, divine love. If we, humankind, as a collective whole would allow Her to make Herself known in consciousness, in the fullness of Her splendor and glory, She would reveal to us and regenerate within us the selfless, compassionate, impersonal, affectionate, uniting side of Her nature – and of ours.

"The Divine Mother speaks to my heart:
'Make room for me;
make womb for me.'
I desire to be one with you."
Priscilla Richards and T.G.B.

Toni G. Boehm

The Feminine Nature of the Divine Who Art Within Me

Exercise:

According to modern day Aramaic researchers, Neil Douglas-Klotz and Rocco Errico, *The Lord's Prayer*, in its original Aramaic wording and context, contains multiple levels of meanings for each word in the prayer. When translated with this idea of multiple levels of meaning, the prayer does not necessarily follow the traditional interpretation that we have used for two millennia. It was from this understanding that the following prayer was birthed.

I invite you to repeat this new version of the prayer, along with the traditional version of The Lord's Prayer (Matthew 6: 9-14 KJV), once per day for next twenty-one days. Repeat them both slowly, first one and then the other. As you do this, you are inviting the energy of the Feminine nature of the Divine to embrace you and to make Herself known to you at the core of your being and you are inviting the Masculine to be present, also. Before long you will feel the presence of both as active energy in your life and affairs and you will feel a sense of balance.

Feminine Nature of the Divine Who Art Within Me

Feminine nature of the Divine
who art within me
And within each living creature,
I celebrate Your numerous
Expressions, names and faces.
Your wisdom flows,
Your love streams forth,
As Your Grace is revealed to me.
Unfolding from the depths within me,
You provide me each day with all I need.
You remind me of my potential.
Your forgiving ways urge me to let go of the strands of false beliefs
That I have held about myself and others.
You support me in knowing my true worth and my inner power.
Your fierceness, courage and loyality underpins my every act.
Thou art my dwelling place,
Yours is the wisdom to know, the power to do,
the love to express, and the joy from which I celebrate.
Now and forevermore this is true.
Ahhh-mmmnn

(Adapted) author unknown

The Traditional Lord's Prayer

Our Father who art in Heaven
Hallowed be thy name
Thy Kingdom come
Thy will be done
On earth as it is in Heaven
Give us this day our daily bread
And forgive us our debts as we forgive our debtors
Leave us not into temptation
But deliver us from Evil
For thine is the Kingdom,
And the Power, And the Glory, Forever
Amen

Mt. 6:9-13

Toni G. Boehm

The Revolution And The Revelation: Where Is She Taking Us Now?

The Revolution

Where is She taking us now? This pure archetypal energy of the Feminine nature of the Divine has been desiring to make Her way back into conscious awareness and to reassert Her values into the conscious mind of humankind ever since Her "banishment" several thousand years ago.

Throughout history, the Divine Mother has exerted Her flame of passion when the time was right – a flame that, when ignited, opened the heart of those willing to surrender to Her love and wisdom, and allowed them to move into a love-in-action mode in the world around them.

On fire with a message that was appropriate to their specific times and culture, the open-hearted ones carried Her message into the world. As Her message, given for a specific time, age, and period of evolution, became absorbed into the consciousness of humankind Her flame would flicker, appear to grow dim, and seemingly disappear.

However, if one looks closely at the events over these past several thousand years, he or she will see that the Feminine's nature of the Divine fiery stream of consciousness has remained eternally. Her face veiled, She has lain in wait ready to flare forth when the consciousness of the humankind was ripe and receptive to Her next series of initiations.

The world appears to be in chaos and extreme turbulence, but I believe that underneath it all is something greater. A revolution of sorts that is trying to emerge. It seems that as a collective society we have chosen pain and suffering as our teachers, for we do not seem to learn without them present as our companions in life. So perhaps the extreme out-picturing of the human condition that humanity is experiencing worldwide is actually our wake-up call – a call "designed," based on our current level of awareness, to create a revolution of consciousness which will move us forward into the next stage of evolution.

She is asking us to take the leap in consciousness. The question is, Will we do it?

The Revelation

The spiritual path is not an easy one. It demands rigor through spiritual practice: devotion through prayer; humility through surrender; and the willingness to endure whatever hardships, "burnings," or crucifixions are placed on our paths in the name of love.

Mary (an expression of the Feminine nature of the Divine) and Jesus (the Christ ideal) came into incarnation at the same time to reveal the true and rightful destiny of humankind. Mary, came not as an idol to be worshiped but as an ideal representing the Divine Feminine, e.g. *"Mary signifies the redeemed feminine, the love power of the soul."*

Mary took incarnation to reveal the importance of the role of the Divine Feminine in the birthing of the Christ consciousness in humanity. Jesus, as the child Mary birthed, came to reveal the Christ consciousness in Its fullest expression in this dimension. His birth and life are referred to as the "first coming" of the Christ consciousness.

Thus, it is only through the intervention of and conscious interaction with the Feminine nature of the Divine (Divine Love, the Holy Spirit) that each person can and will become prepared in consciousness for "the second coming of Christ," the personal experience of birthing the Higher Consciousness, the Christ Presence within them. Together the two of them, Mary and Jesus, unveil the path of love-in-action.

The Divine Mother, in tandem with the Divine Father, creates the sacred Child, the Christ consciousness that lives in you and through the power of that energy of love-in-action you are being asked to *"exert every effort of will and imagination to alter permanently the conditions of life on earth"* (Andrew Harvey, *Mary's Vineyard*).

Discover your sacred purpose, which is to birth the fullness of a greater awareness of the One Power and Presence, and you will be led to your sacred mission. But in order to birth this consciousness, you must be willing to participate in the following: 1. practice sacred disciplines; 2. stand for what you believe in; 3. dedicate your life to the upliftment of humanity by willingly traversing the sacred path; 4. serve humankind in whatever way you are guided; take extraordinary measures (perhaps even revolutionary measures) to ensure that the world will survive and grow into the consciousness that it is destined to express.

I will end this chapter with a quote from Fillmore. It comes from his lecture entitled *"Transmutation."* I believe it speaks to the question Where is She taking us now? This is because the next step on our spiritual journey appears to be the conscious willingness to reach into the depths of our subconscious mind and do the work that prepares the way for a deeper initiation into the activity of the Holy Spirit, through us.

This Holy Spirit movement sets into motion within the cellular structure of the body the regenerative activity that will eventually transform our consciousness into the true spiritual image and likeness of God. Fillmore summarizes succinctly the importance of the work of the Divine Feminine in this process of regeneration. He says:

"If you will go down into your sub-conscious [the feminine aspect of mind] *where you will find Mary, the soul, she will tell you the way. But, each must get busy, and do the work for himself ... The Spirit of the soul in you knows intuitively that you can bring about the transformation, and it is saying constantly ... to the servants* (the servants represent the soul forces, the elemental forces of the organism).

"They [the servants] *are constantly carrying forward the work. This intuition* [the Divine Feminine working in you, guiding you], *if you would give it the opportunity, if you will set it free, will set into activity for you, through all your acquisitions in it, all these powers that will transform and bring about the new mind and the new body. Then, listen to your intuition; get still and hold that you are willing that this transformation, the transmutation of soul and body, should go forth and be fulfilled in you, through the power of the Holy Spirit."*

It is only through the regenerative and restorative power and activity of the Holy Spirit (the Divine Mother, the Divine Feminine), which is "alive" in you, that you will ever have the opportunity to birth the fullness of the mystical Christ consciousness, for without Her all your efforts will be but an intellectual pursuit. In order to create and birth the fullness of all that you desire, the Divine Masculine aspect of God (the intelligence and will) must have as a partner its counterpart, the Divine Feminine, for the only way that the kingdom will come on earth, that the New Jerusalem will be established, is if the Divine Mother in all Her glory and with all Her gifts is brought back into the conscious awareness of humankind.

Call Her and She will make Herself known to you through a quickening that you feel in the midst of Her womb, your heart. She will bless you with Her presence and propel you forward on your journey to freedom. Be willing to enact Her love in the world through the only vehicle She has – **you!**

✺ Epilogue ✺

The End Or The Beginning? The Choice is Always Yours

An epilogue is an ending or addendum that summarizes the concepts and views the author has been subscribing to throughout the book and gives a sense of the possibilities for the future. To do this, I would like to share three streams of thoughts with you. The first and third streams provide a summary of what I believe regarding what has happened over the centuries, with the Feminine nature of the Divine and the consciousness of humankind, and recommendation as to what we can each do to herald in of the next phase of conscious evolution. The second stream is the *"The Mother's Ten Sacred Suggestions"* from *The Return of the Mother* by Andrew Harvey.

Her Flame Of Passion Remained Ignited

There are many that believe that when the feminine nature of the Divine was banished into exile several thousand years ago, Her energy left the Earth. However, I do not believe that Her sacred energy ever left. I believe that throughout history the Feminine nature of the Divine has been exerting Her flame of passion, whenever humankind was ready for a major change in consciousness.

When the flame of the Divine Mother is ignited, it burns open the hearts of those willing to surrender to Her Love and then moves them into a Love-in Action mode in the world around them. Thus on fire with a message that is appropo to the time and culture, the chosen ones carry Her message into the world. Once Her specific message is absorbed into consciousness, Her flame then flickers, appears to grow dim, and seems to disappear back into the "ethers."

If one looks closely at the events that have occurred over the past several thousand years, one will see that the fiery stream of consciousness of the feminine nature of the Divine has remained eternally lit. It lies in wait always ready to flare when the consciousness of the people is receptive to Her next series of transformations. I believe the Divine Mother's cycles of major events chronologically summarized, look (something) like this:

Toni G. Boehm

*35000 B.C.E., the people of the world championed, honored and worshiped in a sense of a Feminine-based spirituality that was inclusive of gender and a sense of equality. The people stood in awe and reverence of the power of a woman to reproduce within herself and then be able to feed that which she had produced – all on her own.

*10000 B.C.E., with the dawn of the Neolithic period came a desire in the people to settle down in one place. This desire spawned the growth of cities and the need for agriculture, rather than hunting and gathering. This "new need" sparked the awareness of husbandry, a required factor in the process of growing plants. With this new awareness "husbandry" came an awareness of the males role in the "creative process" of birthing. Feminine-based spirituality begins to shift slightly, for during this Neolithic period, on occasion, instead of a feminine God standing alone, there are now drawings of both a masculine and feminine form of God– depicted in the form of a pair of animals.

*4500 B.C.E., with the advent of metal everything changes. Indo-European invaders desiring to conquer, possess and establish their beliefs in new domains, used the metal to make weapons and shoe horses. This allowed them to conquer and take control of the "less thans" and to establish a new religion, one that had a concept of a vengeful, male-only God.

*3000– 500 B.C.E., the Great Mother and Goddess tradition continued to thrive in China, Mexico, Africa, Egypt, Greece and etc.. She was known as "The One With a Thousand Names."

*1500 B.C.E., Abraham, the Patriarch of Judaism, the father of the chosen ones, established a new religion and a new covenant.

*600 B.C.E., the Greek mathematician, Pythagorus coined the word, philosophy, "love of Sophia." His intention for the study of philosophy, was that the student would turn inward to the Divine Mother, seeking their inner Wisdom.

*500 B.C.E., a Greek, Heraclitus of Ephesus, shares his teachings on the Logos. He considered the Logos to be eternal and the One through whom all things were made. This concept of the Logos was symbolized by the element of fire and was not gender specific. Thus in the beginning the Logos was genderless and was not a Judaic concept, but Greek.

*400 B.C.E., Sophia, Goddess of Wisdom, is named as a hypostate of God within the Judaic religion. She grew in stature and importance among the people of the Judaic religion. Sophia's role was written about in

Proverbs, Ecclesiastes, Ben Sirach, Wisdom of Solomon, and etc.

*100 B.C.E.(?), Sophia reveals Herself to King Solomon. Solomon wrote about their relationship in the Wisdom of Solomon.

*4 B.C.E.- 1 C.E. (date unknown); Jesus is born and begins his mission of evolving into the Christ consciousness. Jesus' message is one that promotes, honors and exemplifies the attributes of the Feminine nature of the Divine. He reveals how the attributes of the feminine nature of the Divine are necessary for "overcoming" the illusion of death and for "finding one's true self." This deeper hidden meaning of His message was not recognized by the masses. However, it was recognized by an early Christian group known as the Gnostics. (According to research done by Dr. Carl Jung, Gnosticism was very ecumenical and elastic in its views. He also referred to the confrontation of the shadow, or the recognizing of the unacceptable parts of ourselves, as a "gnostic process.")

During this same time a philosopher, and misogynist, named Philo of Alexandria, took the attributes that had been given to Sophia and began, through his writings, to transfer them to Jesus Christ and proclaimed that He was the Logos. He took the Greek genderless concept of the Logos, changed its dynamics and definition and transformed it into the Christian concept of a masculinized Christ.

*33 C.E., it is claimed that Mary Magdalene left Jerusalem after Christ's death, with Joseph of Arimathea, and fled to Egypt. In Egypt Mary Magdalene continued to teach for a few years, after this she (and Joseph) went to France to spread the Good News in Europe. It is also said that Mary, the Mother of Jesus, left Jerusalem with John the disciple and went to Ephesus, Turkey.

*100 C.E., Gnosticism was flourishing, it continued to teach and support the idea of a "hidden wisdom." This wisdom lives within each person and needs no intermediaries for discovery. Gnosticism promoted women as disciples and teachers of the Way, Mary Magdalene was believed to be a Gnostic.

*215 C.E., Mani, the Persian prophet was born. He started a religion that was the principle carrier of Gnoticism for centuries. (It is believed that the French Cathars, Albigensians and the Balkin Bogomils were offshoots of this branch of Gnosticism. Each is said to have helped to reinforce the Gnostic tradition, although, they were forced to go underground with their teachings.)

Toni G. Boehm

*312 C.E., Emperor Constantine is converted to Christianity and declares Christianity to be the religion of the state. Thus the exoteric message of Christianity began to spread and the flame of Gnosticism, the esoteric branch of Christianity, appeared to be headed for extinction.

*325 C.E., the Council of Nicea meets and the doctrine and dogma of Christianity is concretized. Sophia- wisdom, re-incarnation, and Gnosticism with its ideas of "hidden wisdom" and the role of women in leadership, are removed from the tenets and tradition of the newly forming religion of Christianity. The repression, suppression and the apparent demise of the feminine nature of the Divine from religion and consciousness, from all outward appearance was complete.

*431 C.E., the Council of Ephesus met and bestowed upon Mary, the Mother of Jesus the title, "mother of God". (This is one of the first ways that the repressed Divine Feminine's shadow began to rear its head, as it leaves the world with a "Virgin" Mother concept and women with a feminine role model that cannot be replicated.) These last two proclamations make a permanent mark in and on the consciousness of humankind regarding the role of women in religion and in society.

*500 C.E., the last Goddess temple is closed.

*541 C.E., the Byzantine Emperor Justinian I instituted the Candlemas festival. It is celebrated on February 2 in honor of the purification of the Virgin Mary according to Jewish law.

*900 C.E., Gnosticism began to re-emerge in France through a group of followers known as the Cathars or Albigensians.

*1100 C.E., the Gothic Cathedrals were commissioned to be built. The Knights Templars were commissioned to design and build these Cathedrals. A form of sacred geometry was utilized in the building. (Sacred geometry is a form of mathematics which incorporates into its structure the balanced energy of the masculine and the feminine. The Knights Templars held the secret doctrine of the knowledge of the importance of the Divine Feminine energies in life and religion.)

*11th and 12th centuries, the Crusades began and Christianity fought for the right to claim Jerusalem as it's own. Simultaneously, the Inquisition started and hundreds of thousands of persons were exterminated, including the French group of the Gnostic Cathars. During the Inquisition, people were stoned, crushed and burned at the stake for holding beliefs that were "in opposition" to the doctrine of the most Holy church and most of those tortured were women. This "feminine holocaust" went on for centuries and heralded in the beginning of the "Dark Ages."

*12th Century, Hildegard of Bingen, a nun and mystic, had several visions of Sophia. From these visions she wrote music, created artwork and literature, to leave as a legacy to the Feminine nature of the Divine.

* 13th Century, many esoteric teachings went underground, they eventually revealed themselves through and as the songs of the Troubadours, the Tarot deck, art, intricate tapestry design and hidden wisdom of alchemy. All of these were the Gnostic discipline of transformation in a more contemporary disguise.

*1405 C.E., the first church built on Russian soil is the Cathedral of Holy Sophia at Novgorod.

*14th–17th Centuries, the Renaissance began and Sophia as the Divine Mother of Learning and Arts came forth as Wisdom's Seven Pillars (see Proverbs–feast of wisdom). Esoterically this is thought to be the seven liberal arts that formed the base of Western Education.

(During this time frame the deep well of the Divine Feminine's truths, provided a stream of consciousness to: Frances Yates who established the Rosicrucian Movement; Paracelsus the Gnostic wanderer who denounced the establishment and its dogma and values; to alchemy which was thriving; and the Hermetic tradition and the Pansophic tradition which was alive and well. It is believed that many of the great thinkers from the Western traditions, from Galileo to Shakespeare, also drank from Her living waters.)

*15th Century, Jacob Boehme, the Father of Sophiology in the West, was born.

*1654 C.E., a flicker of Light revealed itself, the Cosmic Mother, in the form of Mary appears to the peasant, Juan Diego, in Mexico. She is known as The Black Madonna and Our Lady of Guadalupe and She comes to bring a message of Love and Hope.

*18th Century and the 1700s, brought forth the budding of Freemasonry, the Illuminati and other branches of alternative spiritual traditions. Also there was the work of Shelley, Blake, and Goethe, just to name a few of the poets that danced within the Mother's embrace.

*1776, the country known as America, through it's founding fathers birthed the Declaration of Independence. A proclamation which announced, that the country was a space that held a consciousness of justice, freedom and liberty for all.

Toni G. Boehm

*19th Century and the1800's, saw the first in a series of apparitions of the Cosmic Feminine, the woman clothed in the sun. The "Virgin Mary" appeared in 1846 in La Salette, France. Many more "Mary" apparitions occur over the next 150 years, each time She appeared Her message contained the same intention – Love me (recognize the importance of The Divine Mother, the Divine Feminine in your soul growth) – Love my Son (open to the Christ in you, it is your hope of glory) – and Love each other.

Her stream of consciousness also lived through poets, writers and musicians such as Wagner, Nietzsche, Kierkegaard, Emerson, Will Rogers and many more.

Dec. 8th, 1854, the Doctrine of the Immaculate Conception was declared by Pius IX. This made Mother Mary's birth, as the daughter of Joachim and Anna, holy and pure.

The mid-1800's and the Victorian era, held in consciousness a great oppression for women, in both marriage and in society. This oppression was not only confined to women but to anyone that was not of the "pure strain" and it would seem that purity was defined by whomever was in power.

The Divine Feminine's appearance in consciousness, from Her first flicker in 1654 to the full stream of consciousness which began flowing in the 1800's, was a dawning of a new Era for humankind. I believe Her Energy as it began its influx into human awareness spawned the signing of the Declaration of Independence, the chaos of the Civil War and the clarity of The New Thought Movement. All of these incidences were meant to plant seeds in the consciousness of humankind that would ripen into the fruits of freedom, equality and inclusiveness for all–regardless of gender, race, creed or religious beliefs. And it has begun its work!

New Thought Movement thinking did begin to shift conscious awareness, it was an avenue that first gave women the freedom to begin to speak freely about their inner thoughts and beliefs. As a result, women, as a reflection of the energy of the archetypal Divine Feminine, started coming into their power. This movement of energy, however, was circulating mainly through white, middle to upper class women. Yet, through this New Thought movement people were beginning to realize their innate divinity, rather than their innate "sin."

*1899, Rudolph Steiner declares the end of the Dark Age, the end of the Age of Kali Yuga. In Russia and Eastern Orthodoxy, Sophiology, was flourishing albeit unknown to the Western mind.

*1900's, early in this twentieth century the "Flappers" arrived. These women united in acting in "outrageous" ways; drinking and smoking in public, moving their bodies in shocking and uninhibited ways through dance, wearing short skirts and exhibiting flagrant behaviors that the establishment did not understand.

The Suffragette Movement came into its own during this time-frame. Women united around the ideas and ideals of their right to vote. The right to vote would assure that women's issues would be considered equal in the political arena.

During this same span of time the Temperance Movement was afoot. One could say that this Movements mission was almost the antitheses of the Flappers but it was a uniting of women for a cause. For the commonality that united all of the women during these "movements" was their desire and willingness to demand that they be recognized for what they believed in.

*1917, the Virgin Mary appears at Fatima, Portugal to three children.

Two World Wars were for fought for freedom during this century. World War I began around 1914 and World War II started in 1938. World War II, after 1941, found a shortage of men to work in the factories and women desiring to come to the aid of their country left their homes to take positions in factories to help shore up the shortage and do their part in winning the war.

*1942, Pope Pius XII consecrates the Catholic Church and the world to Mary's Immaculate Heart.

*1945, August 6th, an atomic bombed was dropped on Hiroshima, Japan. World War II ignited the Divine Feminine's energetic flame in a big way, but not necessarily a good way. I believe that the explosion of the nuclear bomb at Hiroshima, sent a shiver down the emotional spine of Mother Earth. If we are a living organism, then so is Earth, and if someone smacked us violently, wouldn't we be shocked? She recoiled and retorted with a statement of, "Enough is enough." This started a major shift in consciousness that would come to full flame in a few short years.

Also, in 1945 the Nag Hammadi Library was found in Egypt, however, it would take 32 years for it to become widely distributed in English. Its discovery and release would cause many to question Christianity (and religion) as it has been taught for over the past 2000 years.

*1947, the Dead Sea Scrolls are found in Qumran, Israel.

*1952, according to author Stephan A. Hoeller, in *The Gnostic Jung*, Dr.

Carl Jung's insights on the shadow and the need in the psyche of humankind for the union of opposites to occur in order to be whole, are considered to be a manifestation of a stream of consciousness of alternative spirituality that descends from Gnostic teachings. Jung, an archaeologist of the soul, never considered Gnosticism, nor its teachings, to be heretical. On Jung's eightieth birthday, the Jung Codex was presented to him, this Codex was the one of the first translations of the Nag Hammadi Library to be viewed outside of Egypt. It is thought that it was Jung's influence and belief in Gnosticism that brought the Nag Hammadi Library out into public prevue.

*1950's, in the late 1940's, and throughout the early 1950's after leaving their jobs in the factories women returned home. But the war had made its mark in consciousness and what women and the world found out was, *"You can take a woman out of the kitchen, but if she goes back, she is probably not going to go back for long."* And so it was with those women who had tasted the freedom of the greater sense of responsibility in the work-place. They had tasted freedom of a pay-check and being their own person–after all the men were gone, that is why they ventured out in the first place—and now it was a part of their consciousness— and they began to get restless. Although, many of those women may not have done anything about this restlessness, they injected something into consciousness that was picked up by the next generation.

*1960's, the 60's, spawned the Peace Movement, which found men and women escaping the confines of home and society in radical way. At this very same time the Civil Right's Movement was being fanned from a spark to a full blown fire. The 60's also gave birth to Barbie, the new role model for young girls, her influence would greatly affect the psyche of women in the years to come.

*1970's, in the 70's, women poured into the work force. There they came face to face with the glass ceiling and a sense of un-equality. Their anger over this and other issues, became the flame that ignited the Feminist Movement and the freedom around "Sexuality" Movement with full force.

During this time the awareness that Earth is the only home we have, generated the feelings that we need to reclaim for Earth, a healthy environment. This generated the Environmental Movement and the Green Peace Movement.

*1980's, June 24th, 1981, St. John's Day, the Virgin Mary appears to six young children in Medjugoric, Yugoslavia and says, *"I am the Queen of Peace."*

During the 1980's, it began to dawn on the many women who had been absorbed into the work-culture, that they were doing double and triple duty. That of mother, wife, worker, cleaner, lover, caretaker and etc. These women began to feel the effects of the *Super-Woman Syndrome*, only they didn't consciously recognize it, they only began to feel it. It would take years for the women to understand what was happening to them on a physical, mental, emotional and spiritual level.

From the Feminist Movement of the 70's a kindling fire ignites and the Goddess Movement comes into vogue. Thousands of women, sick, tired and disillusioned with the patriarchal dogmatic doctrine of religion began choose to return to a more feminine, earth-based spirituality. It was their way of rebelling.

*1989, October 3rd, the Berlin Wall is dismantled.

*1991, Russia institutes a democracy.

*1990's, Seeds previously sown began to burst forth in the 1990's, as major conferences, workshops, retreats and seminars were held for women about women. Women began to feel the freedom to express their concerns for their body, mind and soul and for each other. Women having "paid their dues," were becoming CEO's of companies and holding positions of power.

Having economic freedom, women formed partnerships that provided help to other women. For example, loans were given to poverty-stricken women in third world countries. Loans that would allow these women to become entrepreneurs, self-sufficient and independent. The experiment worked, a 99.9% pay-back of the loans given was received.

The 1990's saw a very a strange phenomenon erupt, it was called the Internet. The Internet is an invisible, mysterious web that interconnects human beings all over the world. Could this Internet, be a covert symbol of the interconnectedness and mysterious aspect of the Divine Feminine coming into awareness? By the end of the 1900's She was starting to move globally.

*2000 C.E., ushered in the new millennium!

October 8th, Pope John proclaimed this next thousand years, the millennium of Mary, which I believe symbolically or esoterically represents a thousand years of the Feminine nature of the Divine at work in human consciousness.

September 11th, 2001, The World Trade Center in New York was attacked by terrorists. Chaos, chaos, chaos, appeared to reign yet from this incident a fierce, protective "Mother-type Energy" emerged revealing a compassionate united America.

With a global focus now emerging, Her Earth is becoming smaller and smaller. However, the environment, pollution, crime, exploitation of children and of women, ethnic cleansing and more, is still going on. The world appears to be in chaos, but underneath it all something greater keeps trying to emerge and perhaps these revelations and movements are a part of Her wake-up call to humankind. But what is She asking us to do? Is She asking to take another leap in consciousness? And if She is, where is She asking us to go or better yet, where is She going to take us? I would invite you to ask yourself these questions, then listen for Her answers and look for the ways you can put Her answers to work in the world.

Leslie Bradshaw

ॐ What Shall We do? ॐ

Andrew Harvey gives us his answers to the question, "What shall we do?"

The Mother's Ten Sacred Suggestions
— Andrew Harve; *The Return of the Mother*

"1. I am the Mother. I am both transcendent and immanent, source and all that streams from it. I am one with all things in creation and one in boundless light within and beyond it. Adore me.

"2. Adore every being and thing, from the whale to the ladybird, as life of my life. I am appearing in everything as everything.

"3. Honor yourself humbly as my divine child, and see, know, and celebrate all other beings as my divine children. Whatever you do to or for anyone, you do to or for me.

"4. See through constant practice of adoration that nature is the sacred body of my sacred light, and do everything at all times to honor its laws that are my laws and to protect it from destruction. I and you and nature are one love, one glory; protecting nature is protecting yourselves.

"5. Dissolve forever all schisms and separations between sects and religions. Whatever you adore is a face of me, and everyone is on his or her own unique path. Know that there are as many paths as there are people.

"6. Dissolve forever through repeated holy inner experience of my unity all barriers between what has been called "sacred" and what has been called "profane." Know the whole of life as my feast. Realize ordinary life as an unbroken flow of normal miracle.

"7. End all hatred of the body … Preserve its purity and power, in my name, with truth and fidelity and mutual honor.

"8. Unlearn all the "religious" propaganda that tries to tell you that you need intermediaries in your relationship with me. I can be contacted by anyone, anywhere, at any time and in any circum-stance, simply by saying my name, however you imagine it. No intermediaries – no gurus, priests, "experts" – are ever needed. You and I are always, already, one.

Toni G. Boehm

"9. Do not make of my worship another dogma, another mind-prison. Remember always there is no "Mother" without the "Father," no "Goddess" without "God." I do not want a new religion in my name; I want the whole of experience on the earth to become holy and integrated in love. I want the return of harmony and sacred peace and balance, the union of the sacred marriage at the greatest depth, and in everyone, of "masculine" and "feminine," "earth" and "heaven," "body" and "soul," heart and intellect, prayer and action. Men are as much my children as women; the wound of the loss of the Mother is felt by women as well as men. Any separatist or prejudiced or one-sided attempt to worship me worships only a distorted image of me. Dare to know me in my full majesty and all-encompassing humility, and know that there is never any end to the journey into me and that the conditions for that journey are ever-deepening faith, radical trust, and radical humility.

"10. If you trust and love me, put your trust and love into action in every aspect of your life – emotional, sexual, spiritual, social, political—with my passion, my clarity, my unsentimental practicality. Know that my revelation is a revolution, a revolution that demands calmly a transformation of all the terms and conditions of life on earth. Establish justice for all in my world, in my name, and in my spirit of all-embracing, inexhaustible compassion. Let no one be poor, or discriminated against, may all sentient beings everywhere be cherished and safe and protected from harm by law and by love. Turn to me now and I will fill you with all the grace, strength, courage, and passion you need to transform the world at every level into a living mirror of my truth, my love, and my justice. If you truly love me, change everything for me."

What Shall We Do? – Integrative Spirituality Requires the Birth of a New Paradigm

To live from a consciousness that contains the spaciousness for Integrative Spirituality (a balanced state of the masculine and feminine aspects of God Energy) will require a major transformation of the mind and heart of each individual and the world in general. Integrative Spirituality as a way of living and being, insists that humankind be willing to birth a new pattern of thinking, feeling and action. This new paradigm holds both the wisdom of knowing and willingness to live in the mystery of not knowing. It is a mind-set that grasps the importance of allowing the activity of the both/and to be guiding force in one's consciousness. We can help to initiate the birth of this new paradigm by:

1. Consciously and intentionally calling forth the feminine nature of the Divine as the next phase of conscious evolution. This phase of conscious evolution is a necessity if we as a species are to advance into living fully from a consciousness of Integrative Spirituality.

2. Being willing to explore the domain of the subconscious mind, Her playground. Once we enter Her domain we will be asked to face our deepest fears for this is the journey that must be taken in order to dance in the fullness of the question, "Who am I ?"

3. Understanding that the pilgrimage into the feminine nature of being necessitates that we embrace our times of chaos, confusion and not knowing, ultimately discerning that these periods are as important to our soul growth as the ones we label "good, pleasant and happy." This is the dance of the both/and. From this state of consciousness (the both/and) we recognize that "birthing pains" or growth pains are a part of the "Feminine/Mother" aspect of nature. This aspect of life cannot be ignored, for pain and birth, go hand in hand. Also, it is important to remember, that in those times when the pain and the anguish of life experiences become unbearable, what is truly happening is that we are in the midst of the possibility of birthing a great awakening. The question is, are we willing to trust, learn and grow from the experience?

4. Remembering that just as birthing is a part of the cycle of life, so is dying. We must learn to engage in and embrace the "dying experiences of our life" as an integral part of transformation. "Dying times," like birthing experiences, are actually stepping stones to a greater awareness of who we are.

Just as the experience of Jesus Christ on the cross, looked like death, what we know now is that it was only an appearance of death. For the true purpose of Jesus` time on the cross was to fulfill his sacred mission – which was to birth humanity into a new level of consciousness. It is only through the appearance of death that we too, are able to birth the true purpose for which we were born. What this means is that the

Toni G. Boehm

results of both dying and birthing are one in the same.

5. Uniting of the head and the heart, the masculine and feminine, thinking and feeling, the conscious (masculine or knowing) and unconscious (feminine or mystery) aspects of mind, is required for soul growth.

6. Recognizing that once the head and heart are united, the heart must then remain open. An open heart is necessary to grow into the wisdom of Integrative Spirituality — prayer and meditation keep the heart open.

7. Trusting and surrendering our will to a Higher Power is imperative for soul growth. Learning to trust the Universal Intelligence and to surrender into It's many disguises and myriad of lessons teaches us that these experiences are merely tests in the school of life and that they have inherent in them the gift of – Wisdom. This Wisdom has within it the ability to "restore the years the locust has taken."

8. Participating in self-observation, self-honesty and the willingness to take authentic action. All of these are requirements for conscious change that leads to transformation, without them change will not lead to transformation.

9. Remembering that we are responsible for our life according to the choices we make. Are you willing to make conscious choices?

10. Realizing that the releasing of attachments to the things of the world, does not mean that you cannot enjoy the things of the world. It means that you do not have to "possess" them.

11. Knowing that compassionate living serves everyone and is the keystone to service in the world

12. Realizing that the Mother is matter, that She is found in the body and in all living things. From this consciousness you will see everything as holy, including yourself.

13. Remembering that we are "wired," **not for** God, but **to be** God-like and all of the above mentioned actions help to establish that connection.

Under this new paradigm we respect the sacred darkness of the subconsciousness mind and use its contents as catalysts to spring-board us to greater awareness` of Self and to living from a consciousness of Integrative Spirituality.

No One But You

I would like to end this book with an adaptation of the Prayer of St. Teresa of Avila that I call;

Leslie Bradshaw

No One But You

The Feminine nature of the Divine has no one but you.

She has no feet, to move forward with, but yours.

She has no eyes to see the injustices in the world with, but yours.

She has no ears to hear the cry of a hungry child with, but yours.

She has no hands to reach out with, but yours.

She has no heart to extend love with, but yours.

She has no lips to pray with, but yours.

She has no body to do Her work in this world, but yours.

Will you take Her messages into the world?

Toni G. Boehm

ᴖ Suggested Readings ᴖ

1. Baigent, Michael, Richard Leigh, Henry Lincoln. *Holy Blood, Holy Grail.* Dell, 1983.

2. Begg, Ean. *The Cult of the Black Virgin.* New York: Penquin, 1985.

3. Boehm. Toni. *One Day My Mouth Just Opened: Reverie, Reflections and Rapturous Musings on the Cycles of a Woman's Life.* Lake Winnebago, Mo.: Inner Visioning Press, 2000. *Embracing the Feminine Nature of the Divine.* L.W. Mo.: Inner Visioning Press, 2000.

4. Butterworth, Eric. *The Universe is Calling.* San Francisco, Ca.: Harper San Francisco, 1993.

5. Braden, Charles. *Spirits In Rebellion.* Dallas, Tx.: South Methodist University Press, 1980.

6. Cole, Susan, Marian Ronan, Hal Taussig. *Wisdom's Feast.* Kansas City: Sheed & Ward, 1998.

7. Cahill, Susan. *Wise Women...*

8. Chamberlain-Engelsmann, Joan; *The Feminine Dimension of the Divine.* Philadelphia, Pa.: Westminster Press, 1979.

9. Charpentier, Louis. *The Mysteries of Chartres Cathedral.* France: Thomson Publishers, 1972.

10. Eisler, Raine. *The Chalice and the Blade...*

11. Fibette, Edith. *Saint Mary Magdalene, Her Life and Times.* Fountain Inn, South Carolina: Society of Mary Magdalene, 1983.

12. Fillmore, Charles. *Archival Sources of Weekly Unity and Sunday Lessons; The Twelve Powers of Man; and The Revealing Word.* Unity Village, Mo.: Unity School of Christianity.

13. Fillmore, Myrtle. *Teach Us To Pray.* Unity Village, Mo.: Unity School of Christianity.

14. Freeman, James Dillet. *Unity Magazine.* Unity Village, Mo.: Unity School of Christianity, May 1987.

15. Gastafason, Fred. *The Black Madonna.* Boston, Ma.: Sigo Press, 1990. (Out of print)

16. Harding, Mary Esther. *Woman's Mysteries.* New York: Harper Colophon, 1972.

17. Harley, Gail M. *Emma Curtis Hopkins: Forgotten Founder of New Thought,* Florida: Unity School Archives, Florida State University, Doctoral Dissertation, 1991.

18. Harvey, Andrew. *Son of Man: The Mystical Path to Christ.* New York: Tarcher Putnam, 1998. *Mary's Vineyard* and *Radiant Heart.* Boulder, Co.: SoundsTrue Tapes, 1998. *The Return of the Mother,* Berkeley, Ca.: Frog Ltd., 1995. Harvey, A. and Eryk Hanut. *Mary's Vineyard,* Wheaton, Il.: Quest Books, 1996.

19. Hopkins, Emma Curtis, *The Ministry of the Holy Mother.* High Watch Fellowship

20. Douglas-Klotz, Neal. *Prayers of the Cosmos.* San Francisco, Ca.: Harper San Francisco, 1990.

21. Lysebeth, Andre Van. *Tantra: the cult of the feminine.* Samuel Weiser Press, 1995.

22. Matthews, Catlin. *Sophia, Goddess of Wisdom.*

23. Mato, Tatayo. *The Black Madonna Within.* Chicago, Il.: Open Court, 1996.

24. Michell, John. *The City of Revolution.* London, England: Garnstone Press, 1971

25. Mollenkott, Virginia Ramey. *The Divine Feminine: the Biblical Imagery of God as Female.* New York: Crossroads, 1994.

26. Myss, Carolyn. *Anatomy of the Spirit.* New York: Harmony Books, 1997.

27. Pagels, Elaine. *The Gnostic Gospels.* Dell Publishing, 1981

28. Powell, Robert. *Trinosophia,* 2000. Tape set, *Sophia's Teachings.* Colorado: SoundsTrue,1998. *Meditations on the Tarot.* translation by R. Powell, Element Books, 1985.

29. QuAlls-Corbett, Nancy. *The Sacred Prostitute.* Inner City Books, 1988.

30. Russell, Peter. *A White Hole In Time.* San Francisco, Ca.: Harper San Francisco, 1992.

31. Stone, Merlin. *When God was a Woman.* Dell Press, 1976.

32. Starbird, Margaret. *The Woman with the Alabaster Jar.* Sante Fe, N.M.: Bear & Co, 1993. *The Goddess in the Gospels.* Sante Fe, N.M.: Bear & Co, 1998.

33. Steiner, Rudolph. *Spiritual Hierarchies and the Physical World.* Hudson, New York:Anthroposophic Press, 1909-1911.

34. Tomberg, Valentine. *Meditations on the Tarot.* Shaftesbury, Dorset: Element Books, 1985.

35. Vahle, Neal. *Myrtle Fillmore: Torch-Bearer To Light the Way.* Unity Village, Mo.: Unity House, 1996.

36. Walker, Barbara. *Women's Rituals* San Francisco, Ca.: Harpers San Francisco, 1983.

ᤌ About the Author ᤍ

Toni G. Boehm is an author, nurse, minister, and teacher of spirituality and mysticism. She is currently the Dean of Administration for Unity School of Religious Studies, Unity School of Christianity, Unity Village, MO. Teaching internationally she facilitates classes and seminars on prayer, prosperity, personal growth and empowerment, awakening the feminine nature of the divine in the 21st Century, and spiritual transformation. She introduces students to the spiritual knowledge and skills necessary for living their lives from their highest innate potential. Her life work is devoted to "being a midwife for the birthing of the soul's remembrance."

Boehm has a Bachelor of Arts in Health Care Education, from Ottawa University-Kansas, a Masters of Science in Nursing, from the University of Missouri, and a Ph. D. from American World University-Iowa.

Prior to joining the staff as dean at Unity School for Religious Studies, Boehm served as senior staff specialist for accreditation and certification for the American Nurses Association and as clinical nurse specialist/manager for the medical department at Hallmark Cards, Inc.

She was the recipient of the University of Missouri- Kansas City, Women's Council Award for Research for her Master's thesis. She is listed in Marquis' *Who's Who in America* and *Who's Who In American Women*.

Boehm is the author of numerous articles and the books, *The Spiritual Intrapreneur; One Day My Mouth Just Opened: Reverie, Reflections and Rapturous Musings on the Cycles of a Woman's Life;* and *Embracing the Feminine nature of the Divine:Integrative Spirituality Heralds the Next Phase of Conscious Evolution*

Toni Boehm has written a one woman play entitled, *Feminine Voices: The Women Who Live In Our Cellular Memories*, she can be contacted for a performance of this play or other events such as; Wisdom Circle retreats; Feminine Wisdom Initiation ceremonies; prayer retreats; keynote addresses; or her Shadow-Dancing workshop at:

**816-304-3044, by fax at 816-537-5254,
by e-mail at Revtboehm@aol.com,
or by writing 430 Winnebago Dr.
Lake Winnebago, MO., 64034, U.S.A.**

To order books or tapes, e-mail or write
Dr. Boehm at the above mentioned addresses.

Note: There is soon to be a study guide available for purchase, to use in self-study or teaching this book as a class.

Printed in the United States
6156

9 780970 153715